DENTISTRY

Cavendish
Publishing
Limited

DENTISTRY

John E Rowson, B Med Sci (Hons), MB, BS, BDS,
FDSRCS, FRCS,
Consultant Maxillofacial Surgeon, Nottingham

Adrian E Slaney, BDS, DRDRCS, FDSRCS (Edin), LLM,
Dental Surgeon
Part-time Hospital Practitioner, West Norwich Hospital

Cavendish
Publishing
Limited

First published in Great Britain 1996 by Cavendish Publishing Limited, The Glass House, Wharton Street, London WC1X 9PX.

Telephone: 0171-278 8000 Facsimile: 0171-278 8080

Slaney, Adrian E

Dentistry for Lawyers – (Medico-legal practitioner series)

1. Dental laws and legislation – England

I Title II Rowson J

617.6'0024344

ISBN 1-85941-212-2

Printed and bound in Great Britain

FOREWORD

Those who have shown an interest in the 'medico-legal practitioner's series' may like to learn something about its origins and the history of its development. With this objective in mind I will devote a few moments to the past and I will then turn to the future which is, after all, even more important for us.

I first conceived the idea of such a theme in the Summer of 1994. By that stage I had been preparing reports for lawyers on cases of alleged medical negligence for about five years. I had also been looking at other doctors' reports for the same length of time and it was becoming increasingly apparent to me that one of the lawyers' most difficult tasks was to understand the medical principles clearly. To be fair to the lawyers, there were some doctors who did not always make matters very clear. This, coupled with the difficulty which many doctors have in understanding the legal concept of negligence and related topics, merely served to compound the problem.

It therefore occurred to me that a possible solution to the difficulty would be to develop some material on medical topics written by doctors who had a particular interest in the medico-legal field. The authors would require at least four attributes. First, they would have to be specialists in their own field. Secondly, they would need the ability to explain their subject to non-medical readers in clear language that was easy to follow. Put another way there was no case for writing a medical textbook for their students or colleagues. Thirdly, they would require a fair amount of experience in medico-legal reporting, analysis of cases and dealing with lawyers who were defending or advancing cases. This would give them an understanding of how the lawyer's mind works and an appreciation of the medical areas which can cause difficulty in practice and where accidents can happen. There would be a contrast with medical books where the emphasis is on the diseases which most commonly present to the doctor. Fourthly, the authors would need the ability to work in harmony with a series editor who was anxious to achieve some degree of uniformity across the whole range of the material.

Having identified these four points as being desirable characteristics of the potential authors the next step was to find a publisher who would be sufficiently interested to give the project the support it needed. This was to be no small task and was likely to involve a very long term commitment because, after the initial launch, it was inevitable that much more work would be required by way of future editions and additional titles. I was most fortunate to be dealing with Cavendish Publishing in connection with my own book, *The General Practitioner and the Law of Negligence,* and I am pleased to say that they seized this new idea with the utmost enthusiasm. At last I thought that the 'medico-legal practitioner series' would become a reality.

It then only remained to find the authors, commission the work and wait for the results. It was at this point, however, that I began to realise that I was still only at the very beginning of my task. Eventually, however, after numerous discussions with various people a team materialised. When the early chapters of the first books began to arrive it was starting to look as though we really were going to have something which was quite unique. When the final manuscripts arrived my confidence increased still further. More than two years after my initial plans the first set of books has become available and the dream has turned into reality.

This, then, is how the project came into being but it must be emphasised that, in a manner of speaking, we have really only just got ourselves started. For the series to thrive it must be flexible and respond to the needs of its users. It must adapt to medical developments and legal changes. Clinical subjects are a primary consideration but it is my firm intention to expand the series to involve other areas of interest. Indeed the first non-clinical title should appear almost as soon as the initial set becomes available. On a more long term basis, I would like the series to cover every field of expertise that is of concern to the medico-legal practitioner.

Uniformity of approach and clarity of presentation must be hallmarks of the individual titles but the series as a whole must be independent and objective. If we can aspire to these criteria we should achieve a fair measure of success in assisting our readers to give good advice to their clients.

It remains for me to express my gratitude to all the authors and to the publishers for their cooperation. In another kind of way I will be equally grateful to all our readers for placing their reliance on us and for sharing our optimism.

Walter Scott
Series Editor
Slough
August 1996

PREFACE

The first task of any aspiring professional is to become acquainted with the terminology of the chosen subject. When the need arises to understand and discuss problems in another professional field, it is, inevitably, the new terminology that forms the largest barrier to communication and which may lead to misunderstanding.

Claims of negligence against the professions have been increasing over the last few years. Lawyers increasingly have to deal with the subject of dental surgery in its widest sense. This requires a basic understanding not only of the terminology, but of the scope of the profession, its relationships and its organisation.

The aim of this book is to provide the reader with a basic explanation of the terms used and the procedures carried out by dental surgeons. It further provides an outline of the necessary sciences relevant to dentistry and of the organisation of dental practice. It is hoped that, with this book, lawyers will be able to understand both terminology and procedures used in all aspects of dentistry.

This work is not intended to be a comprehensive textbook, of which there are many for each area of dentistry. It provides a guide for those who find themselves involved in dento-legal work and wish to gain some knowledge and understanding of the dental profession and the range of treatment in and around the oro-facial complex.

John E Rowson
Adrian E Slaney
August 1996

CONTENTS

CHAPTER ONE

HISTORICAL PERSPECTIVE

From the earliest times the Ancient Egyptians used a variety of remedies to treat diseases of the mouth. Around 2000BC the Chinese described toothache and gum diseases, while around 400BC Hippocrates described various forms of dental treatment in use during the Greek civilisation period. During the 1st century AD, Celsus described the art of tooth extraction undertaken in the Roman empire.

In the Middle Ages tooth extractions were carried out by barbers, and by the 14th century they had formed guilds, each with their own list of members and sets of rules appertaining to general conduct. This was a time when trade guilds were rapidly developing and the Guild of Barber-Surgeons was one of many. The number of barber-surgeons was small and largely limited to large towns and cities, thus leaving the rural population devoid of this amenity. This eventually led to the so-called 'itinerant tooth-drawers' who travelled throughout the country areas visiting towns and villages solely for the removal of teeth in the local population. These often flamboyant characters advertised their 'trade/occupation' by wearing colourful hats and necklaces made of strings of teeth. Many of these tooth-drawers regularly set up pitches at fairs and markets throughout the country areas.

During the mid-18th century the term 'dentist' appeared, its linguistic origins being French. The dentists of this period had extensive skills ranging from extractions to simple restorative procedures such as fillings and the treatment of gum disease. The need for their services grew during the 18th century as a result of the increase in sugar consumption, albeit an expensive commodity. For hundreds of years decay resulting in toothache was believed to be caused by a worm living in the teeth.

Until about 1770 the practice of dentistry was either a trade or simply an occupation carried out by people who were often illiterate and completely lacking in any form of medical education or practical skills relating to tooth extraction. No doubt some of the itinerant 'tooth-drawers' had acquired some knowledge from books and pamphlets, but the majority gained their experience from being taught the practical skills by fellow 'tooth-drawers'. Towards the end of the 18th century there existed a variety of people carrying out the practice of dentistry, largely made up of itinerant 'tooth-drawers', a small number of 'barber-surgeons' and 'dentists'.

In 1745 the 'surgeons' formally separated from the 'barbers', but it wasn't until 1800 that the Royal College of Surgeons was finally granted its charter.

The 'dentists' were a small group, probably working from the larger population centres where they would carry out various dental procedures including the provision of artificial teeth. There was no proper training, although no doubt a few would take on young lads for four or five year apprenticeships. There was at this time no professional body to monitor training or provide any examinations or licences.

The majority of 'dentists' practising in the UK during the 19th century were lacking in scientific knowledge. Many of these were drawing an income from another trade or profession, practising 'dentistry' as a sideline by putting up a sign and hailing themselves as a 'surgeon-dentist'. With no formal training or registration the practice of dentistry was open to charlatans who could exact a great deal of damage on their patients without redress to any formal body such as the Royal College of Surgeons or the General Dental Council.

A young Croydon dentist, one Samuel Lee Rymer, in a letter published in the *Lancet*, in August 1855, suggested that an examination leading to a diploma should be instituted by the College of Surgeons. He spoke of:

> '... the suffering, a loss (both in teeth and pocket) from the ignorance and extortion of the exposed dentist. I can speak from experience as to the roguery (for that is not too strong a word) of a very large number of men who call themselves dentists but who are in reality wholly ignorant of the surgical anatomy of the mouth and parts adjacent as well as the principles (to say nothing of the practice) of mechanisms as applied to dentistry. No wonder such men are the origin of so much disappointment, pain and, I believe, death.'

He went on to suggest the establishment of a dental school and a college of dental surgery with a board of examiners. Rymer was to play an important role in consolidating the practice of dentistry, raising the standards of education and ethics as well as elevating its standards to a more professional level.

In September 1859 the royal assent was given for a dental charter to be instituted together with a board of examiners provided by the Royal College of Surgeons (s 48 of the Medical Act 1858). Proposals were also made which involved the award of diplomas under the auspices of the Royal College of Surgeons. The latter held its first examinations for the Licentiate in Dental Surgery (LDS RCS) on 13 March 1860.

It wasn't until 1878 that the first Dental Act was passed by way of rigorous campaigning by a small group of dentists, one of whom was John Tomes (later Sir John). Unfortunately there were inherent weaknesses in the drafting of the Act insofar as it was unable to put an end to unregistered dental practice. Section 3 merely stated that any unregistered person who adopted the title of 'dentist' or 'dental practitioner' would be punished. Providing the above titles were not adopted the unregistered dentist could safely practice without any fear of being prosecuted. Three groups of persons were eligible for registration under s 6 of the Act:

(a) licentiates in dental surgery or dentistry of any of the medical authorities;

(b) foreign or colonial dentists; and

(c) persons bona fide engaged in dental practice, either separately or in conjunction with the practice of medicine, surgery or pharmacy.

The first dentists register was published in 1879 and administered by the General Medical Council. The register included all those who had been practising dentistry before the Act as well as the qualified practitioners. Any future registrations would only include those who had graduated with the Licentiate in Dental Surgery. Acquiring registration entitled each member to adopt the title 'dentist' or 'dental surgeon'.

Complications associated with the interpretation of the Act and the exploitation of its loopholes created serious difficulties for the General Medical Council and the British Dental Association (set up in 1880), particularly where they had to determine whether to enter any given name in the dentists register. For example:

> 'Christian Ackermann, number 88 Victoria Dock Road, Canning Town, London, was summoned to appear and did appear before this Council on the 29th day of October last, when, on examination, it appeared: "that he was a native of Brandenburg, in Germany, an apprentice to learn hairdressing in his own country where they always learn dentistry and dressing in the general way, taking blood, putting leeches on and extracting teeth. After apprenticeship, served three years in the German army as a dresser in a hospital. Produced his testimonials. Now carries on the business of a hairdresser and dentist at the above address and has been there five years. Admitted ignorance of the anatomy of the mouth. Does nothing but extract teeth. Extracted last year 612 teeth, the year before something over 500. Wife has a tobacco counter in the shop. Has his name as 'registered dentist' painted on a tablet outside his shop window."'

Examples of these cases were commonplace during the early years before the passing of the Dentists Act.

Section 6 of the Act failed to provide any minimum period prior to registration and also failed to provide any advice as to how long a person should have been engaged in the practice of dentistry before he could be registered. The initial rush to register was beyond expectation and numerous difficulties arose, which gave the Registrar a great deal of anxiety. This included difficulties in deciphering names and addresses, and forms returned incorrectly filled in. The Registrar also found a number of persons attempting to register who were children, while others had attempted to register who had passed retirement age. With no legal requirement to register, many considered it unnecessary to do so. Provided they did not use the titles protected under the Act, it was possible to continue to practice without any formal education or ethical standards.

In 1917 the Government set up a departmental committee:

> '... to enquire into the extent and gravity of the evils of dental practice by persons not qualified under the Dentists Act 1878.'

The report was published in 1919 and its findings were accepted by the Government, and finally led to the Dentists Act 1921 which closed up the loopholes that existed in s 3 of the 1878 Act.

Rymer was the original instigator of 'dental professionalism' but it took 66 years between 1855 and 1921 before dentistry could be considered to have achieved complete professional status. This led to a new era in dental practice which then rapidly improved throughout the 20th century, taking public confidence with it.

CHAPTER TWO

THE DENTAL SURGERY

The dental practice is made up of the dental surgeon(s) and their respective dental surgery assistants (DSAs). Many practices also employ hygienists whose role is to provide oral hygiene instruction and to carry out scaling and polishing. They are involved in giving dietary advice and applying fluoride. Some practices still employ dental technicians on the premises although the numbers are falling, and in today's modern practices most impressions taken of the teeth for the construction of dentures, crowns, bridges and orthodontic appliances are sent out to a laboratory of choice.

A receptionist and sometimes a practice manager, who maintains the everyday function of the practice, are also employed, especially in multiple practices employing a large number of clinicians and ancillary personnel.

THE SURGERY

Modern day practices usually consist of:

(a) fully reclining dental chair;

(b) two mobile chairs, one for the DSA who usually sits on the left hand side of the patient and one for the dentist sitting on the right hand side;

(c) wall to wall cabinets with individual wash basins and easy access to instruments and materials;

(d) illumination by way of an operating light;

(e) high speed turbine drills which require water cooling. The water needs to be collected, and so high powered suction is available to remove debris, excess saliva and the cooling water;

(f) an air/water syringe used to dry cavities and to wash out debris;

(g) possibly a spittoon for rinsing, although with close support dentistry and high speed suction utilised by the DSA the need for spittoons has been greatly reduced;

(h) eye protection using plastic eyeglasses to protect the patient, especially in the supine position when they are susceptible to instruments and materials being dropped, and for the clinician as protection against debris and contaminated water droplets from the high speed cutting instruments passing into the eyes;

(i) a wall mounted X-ray unit;

INFECTION CONTROL

Patients and staff should be protected from infection. Infection can be transmitted from the patient to staff or visa versa, or from patient to patient (cross-infection). All instruments used for a specific patient should afterwards be thoroughly cleaned and wire-brushed to remove all debris, eg cement, before being sterilised in an autoclave. All work surfaces should be scrupulously clean, and a variety of proprietary materials are on the market for maintaining clean work tops and dental equipment. Any spilt blood or pus should be cleaned with disinfectant containing hypochlorite solution or 2% gluteraldehyde.

The routine use of gloves by the clinician and the DSA is highly recommended to prevent the transmission of infection from the patient to the dental team, with particular relevance to the viruses responsible for hepatitis and the acquired immunodeficiency disease syndrome (AIDS) which may be transmitted in blood or saliva. With known carriers of the relevant viruses special precautions can then be taken to treat these patients. Their treatment is usually undertaken at the end of a session so that, after the procedure, the surgery can be thoroughly disinfected and the relevant disposable items sealed in yellow plastic bags for immediate disposal and incineration. With these patients it is normal practice to wear full protective clothing which should be disposable. All instruments should be thoroughly scrubbed before being autoclaved.

WASTE DISPOSAL

All sharp items including needles, scalpels and local anaesthetic cartridges should be placed in a rigid, well marked container. Other clinical waste from cotton wool rolls to swabs and tissues should be sealed in a stout, plastic bag. Arrangements should be made for this clinical waste to be disposed of either by taking the waste to the local hospital or arranging a suitable collection service at regular intervals. All clinical waste should be separate from ordinary domestic waste.

SAFETY AND SECURITY

Other potentially dangerous materials, eg mercury, are also used. Therefore practices need to conform to COSHH (control of substances hazardous to health) regulations, and any potentially dangerous materials must be labelled. For example acrylic resin liquid, which is used to construct the plastic base plates for dentures and can be used by the dental surgeon for repairing dentures in the practice, is highly inflammable, while hypochlorite or bleach can cause burns if handled carelessly. Various drugs are used and some are classified as 'dangerous drugs'; strict laws govern their storage and use. Few practices keep such drugs (eg morphine), but if they are kept they must be in a locked cupboard with access only to authorised key holders. These drugs can only be dispensed by the dentist and a log book must be kept of the patient's name, quantity dispensed and current total stock.

PRACTICE INSPECTIONS

From 1 April 1992 FHSAs (Family Health Service Authorities)* have had the power to inspect the premises of any dentist on their list. These inspections will only be carried out by general dental practitioners appointed by the FHSA as its dental advisors. In addition, one other person from the FHSA is allowed to visit with the inspecting practitioner but only for administrative and observational purposes, leaving the reports to be carried out by the practitioner only. The inspecting practitioner will look at the premises and the equipment. He will have a basic check list and will inspect the general standard of decor, cleanliness and facilities, eg toilets. Equipment and instruments will be inspected for cleanliness as well as the cross infection controls present in the practice environment. Other health and safety requirements will also be checked to ensure that standards are satisfactory.

If the results of the inspection are unsatisfactory action may be taken; much depends on the seriousness of the problems noted at the time of the inspection, but normally these will be minor and a letter to the dentist explaining the problems will be carried out by the general manager of the FHSA and followed up with a further visit a couple of months later. Disciplinary action may be taken, although before this is carried out it will be necessary to ask a dental reference officer from the Dental Practice Board (DPB) to carry out a separate report. If this is still unfavourable then it is this report which will be used in any service committee disciplinary action.

*From 1 April 1996 these have been merged with local health authorities who are now responsible for all aspects of the health of the population in the area they cover.

CHAPTER THREE

ANATOMY OF THE HEAD AND NECK

It is not within the scope of this chapter to detail the whole of the anatomy of the human head and neck. There are many excellent standard anatomical textbooks to which reference can be made for such details. The purpose of this section is to provide a general overview of the anatomy of the region.

BONE STRUCTURE

The bones of the head and neck may be conveniently divided into four groups. The cranium provides a large, enclosed space containing the brain. There are many holes in this box that transmit the nerves, via which the brain communicates with the rest of the body, and the vessels supplying the brain with nutrients and removing its waste products. In addition, there are two smaller cavities anteriorly in which the eyes (that are really projections of the brain) are encased.

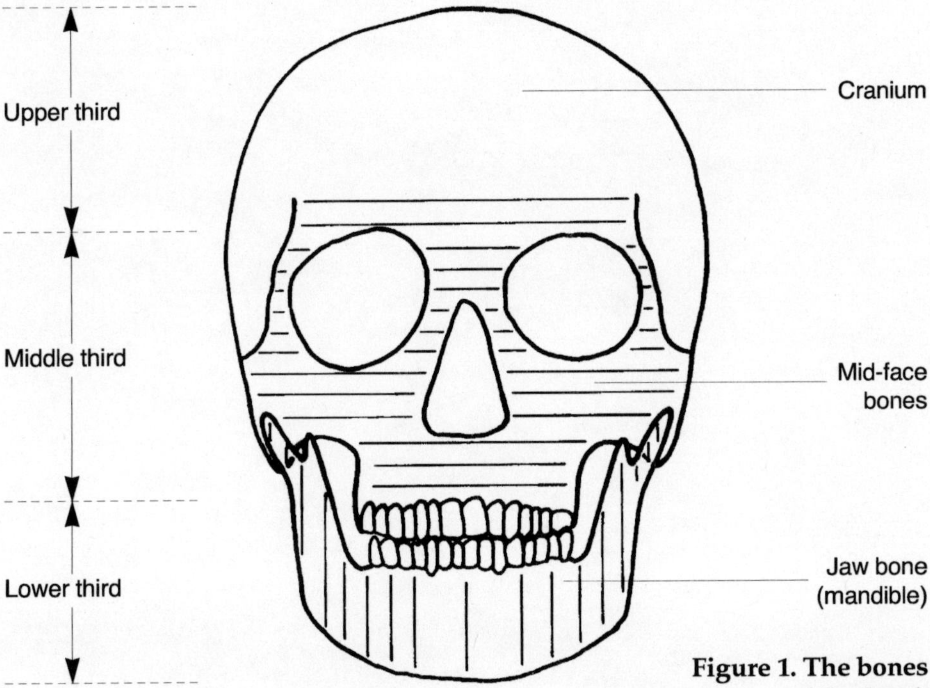

Figure 1. The bones of the head.

The second group of bones forms the delicate structure of the face below the cranium including the upper jaw, the nose, and cheek bones containing spaces forming part of the upper airways. The third part, the mandible (lower jaw), is hinged to the skull via two joints, the temporomandibular joints. The lower jaw and upper jaw hold the teeth and together form the masticatory (chewing) mechanism. The fourth group of bones are those forming the top part of the spinal column in the neck on which the head rests.

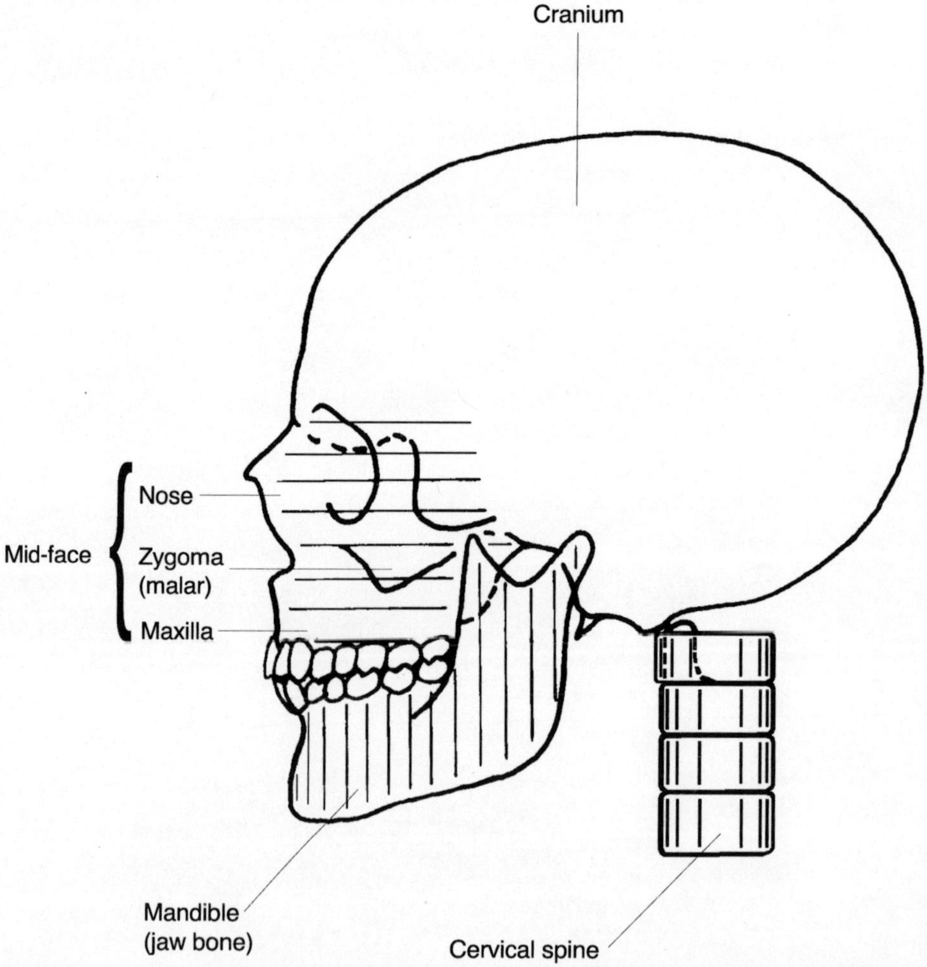

Figure 2. The bones of the head and neck.

The bones with which we are concerned in the field of dentistry are mainly restricted to the lower jaw (mandible), the upper jaw (maxilla), the cheek bone (zygoma or malar) and the bones forming the palate.

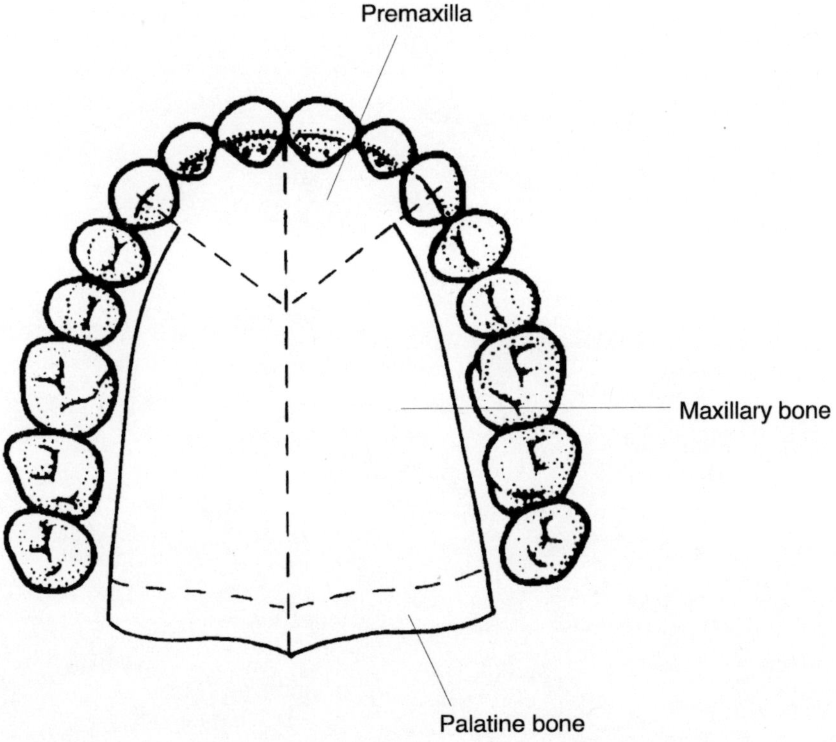

Figure 3. The hard (bony) palate and upper teeth.

The upper jaw has an anterior section containing the incisor teeth called the premaxilla which develops as a separate unit in early growth. Behind this the paired maxillae contain the rest of the teeth and are joined at the mid-line by fibrous joint that later becomes bony. Behind these, forming the rest of the palate, are the palatine bones. On the lateral aspect of the maxillae the zygomatic bones are attached, again by a fibrous joint that later becomes bony. These bones form the prominence of the cheek. Within the maxilla and zygoma below the floor of the orbit there is a large space called the maxillary sinus (antrum). This sinus sits above the roots of the teeth and constitutes an important anatomical relationship (Figure 4).

Each sinus lies adjacent to the side of the nasal cavity and is connected to it via a small gap in the intervening wall.

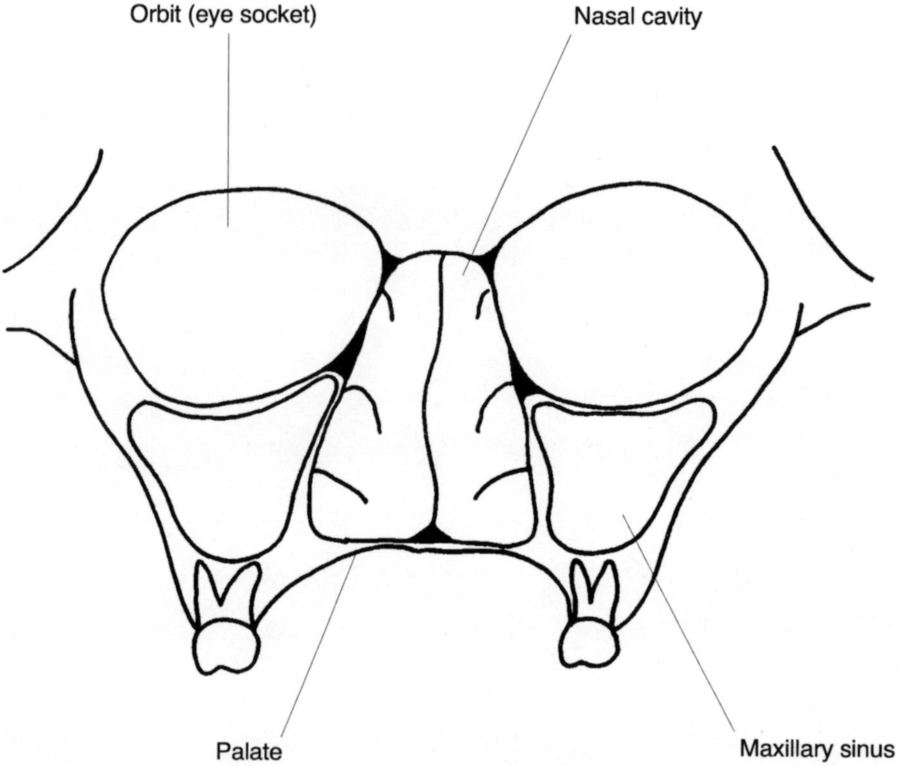

Figure 4. A cross-section through facial bones at the level of the molar teeth.

The mandible develops in two halves which fuse early in life, so forming one discrete bone attached to the base of the skull via the two temporomandibular joints, and has a special relationship with the maxilla via the teeth. The mandible is a dense bone and is relatively strong. It may conveniently be divided into four parts for description (Figure 5).

Firstly, there are the processes forming the temporomandibular joint. These joints are complex but basically represent a hinge within a socket on the base of the skull which is designed to slip out of the sockets slightly to allow lateral and rotary movements as used in chewing. These processes (condyles) do not rest directly on the base of the skull since there is a fibrous disc (meniscus) securely attached to the condyles dividing each temporomandibular joint into two joint cavities (*qv* Chapter 16).

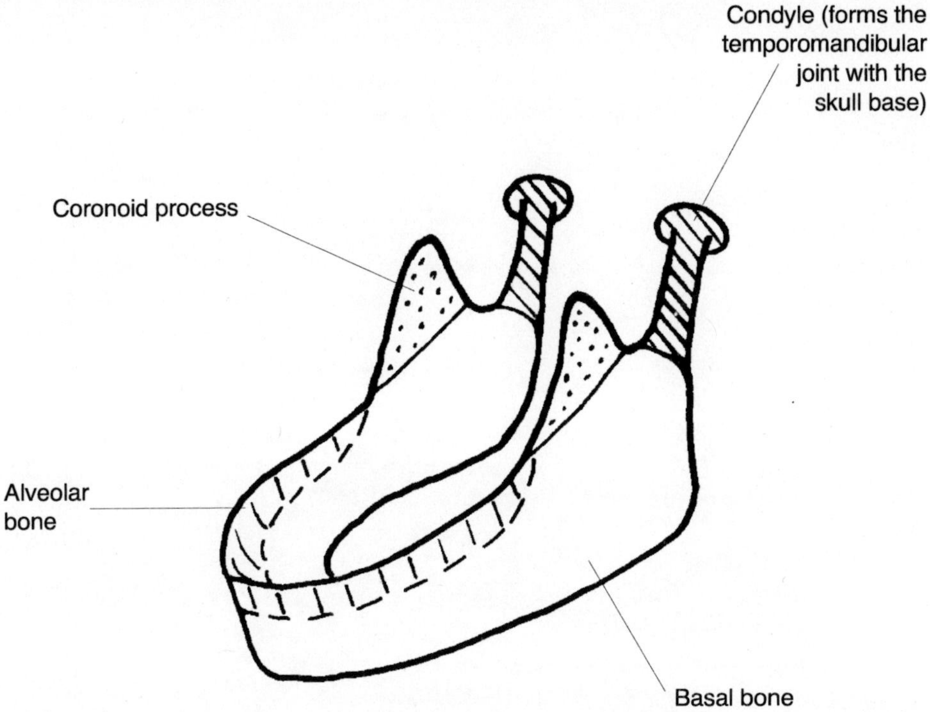

Figure 5. The mandible.

The second part of the bone is the large process on which some of the main muscles for closing the jaw are attached – the coronoid processes. These lie just in front of the condylar processes and give attachment to the temporalis muscle, which will be described later. The third part is the main arch of the jaw, called the basal part of the mandible. The fourth part is the bone which sits on the third part and supports the teeth, and is called the alveolar process.

An important anatomical feature of the mandible is a canal lying within its body. This contains a nerve (inferior dental/inferior alveolar nerve) that supplies sensation to the lower teeth and, via a branch (mental nerve) that leaves the jaw between the premolar teeth, supplies the lip. It also contains an artery and vein which help supply the mandible and teeth. Although this nerve is normally well protected by being within bone it is obviously at risk if the bone is fractured and when certain procedures are carried out, eg extraction of third molar teeth.

MUSCULATURE

There are many muscles in the head and neck; however, only a few of these have relevance to dentistry. The muscles of mastication are a group of muscles which control jaw movement. The largest in size and number are those which close the jaw giving power to the bite. These include the temporalis muscle, which is a large muscle attached to the side of the skull passing downwards to its insertion on the coronoid process of the mandible previously described. In addition, two other powerful muscles take origin from the base of the skull and the rear portion of the cheek bone, and these pass down on each side of the mandible and are attached over a large area around the angle of the mandible. These are, on the outer side, the masseter and, on the inner side, the medial pterygoid.

There is a large sheet of muscle attached to each side of the mandible anteriorly which forms the floor of the mouth and is called the mylohyoid. The other important muscle masses in this region are the buccinator muscle, which is the muscle of the cheek, and the group of muscles which make up the mass called the tongue. The tongue in anatomical terms is simply a large group of muscles which act in various directions, so making the tongue an extremely mobile organ.

Figure 6. The main muscles of mastication (the medial pterygoid is on the inside surface of the mandible and is not shown).

BLOOD SUPPLY

The head has one of the best blood supplies of any area of the body. It is richly supplied with vessels which comprise all the branches of the external carotid artery, which itself is a branch of the common carotid artery in the neck. The facial, lingual and maxillary arteries are the main branches which supply the face and mouth and they have many anastomosies (junctions), and therefore form a complex network of vessels around this area. The blood is drained from the area by veins which form a complex anastomosis of vessels, but drain via larger veins, accompanying the main arteries, into the jugular vein in the neck (Figure 7).

SALIVARY GLANDS

The skin lining of the mouth (mucous membrane) contains many tiny glands which contribute to the saliva within the mouth. In addition to these small glands, there are three pairs of major salivary glands as follows.

(a) Parotid glands – these lie behind the mandible, spread out onto the side of the face in front of the ear and contribute a large volume of saliva via a duct opening next to the upper second molar tooth.

(b) Submandibular glands – these lie in the floor of the mouth against the inner surface of the body of the mandible posteriorly. They drain via ducts in the floor of the mouth opening near the mid-line under the anterior aspect of the tongue, behind the lower front teeth.

(c) Sublingual glands – smaller than the others, they lie in the anterior region of the floor of the mouth and open via a number of small ducts into this area.

Altogether the various salivary glands produce a potential 1–1.5 litres of saliva a day. This has a number of very important functions including lubrication, cleansing and protection against infection. In recent times it has become more important in forensic dentistry since various blood group factors are found in the saliva (Figure 8).

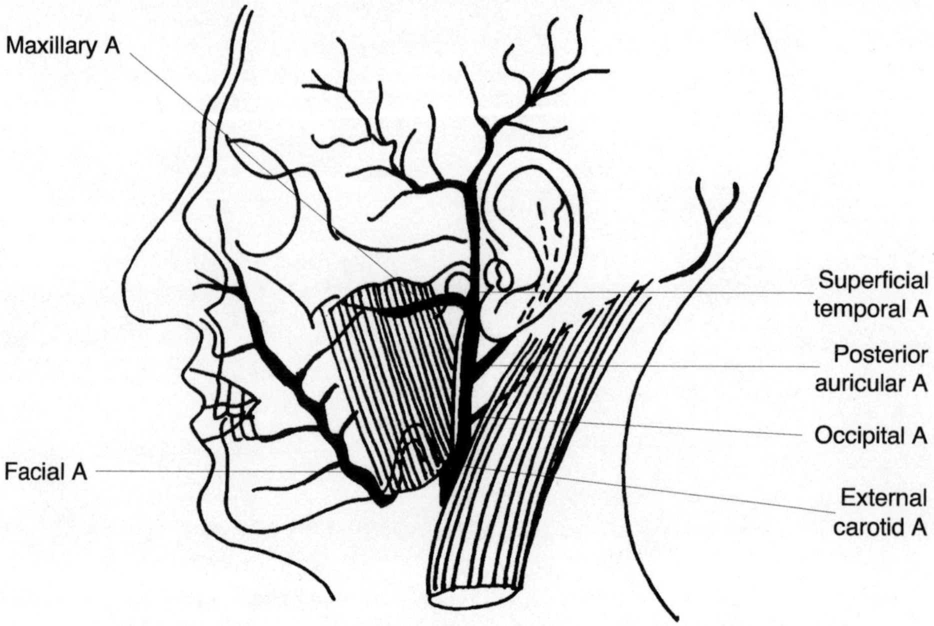

Figure 7. The main arteries of the face.

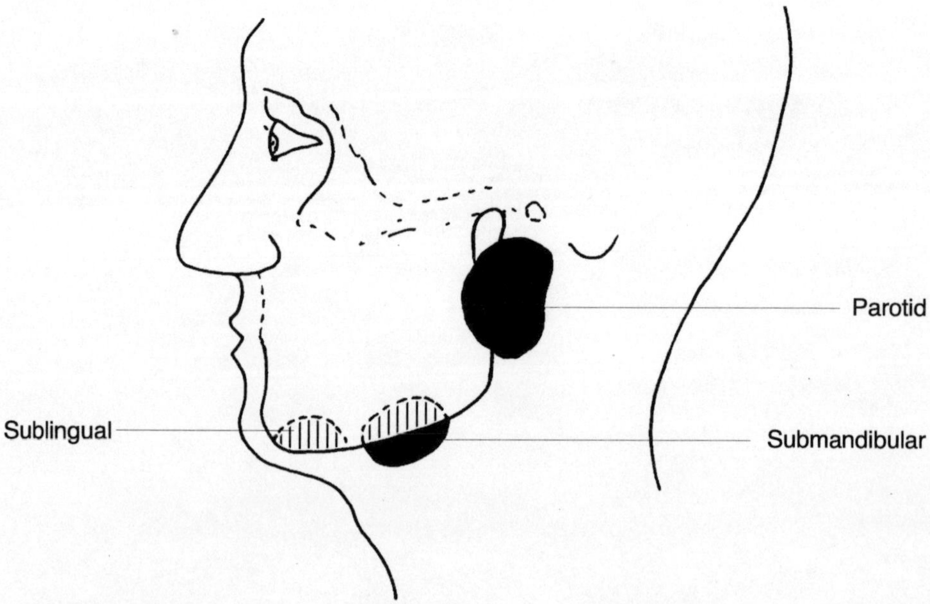

Figure 8. The main salivary glands.

THE SOFT PALATE

This is a flap of soft tissue behind the bony palate and its function is to seal off the oral cavity from the nasal cavity during swallowing to prevent reflux of food into the nose. It also has an important function in speech, and damage may cause a disturbance of speech due to the escape of air.

TONGUE

The tongue has many functions. It is important in swallowing, speech, taste and in general cleansing of the mouth. It contains nerves for general sensation and for specific sensations associated with taste of sweet, sour, salt and bitter flavours. Damage to the nerve (lingual nerve) which transmits general sensation and special taste sensations may therefore lead to considerable disability.

NERVE SUPPLY

There are two broad types of nervous system within the body;

(a) the somatic, which gives rise to skin sensation and conscious muscular movement; and

(b) the autonomic, which controls body homeostasis and supplies the internal organs of the body.

In the region we are dealing with the somatic nervous system is the one with which we are mainly concerned. One can think in simple terms of the human body developing from a more simple form based on an earthworm. This creature is divided into segments, each possessing a muscle for movement and a sensory organ giving information about the external environment. Each segment therefore, has its own motor and sensory nervous supply.

The human body can, likewise, be divided into segments. Each with its own motor and sensory supply. In the trunk these nerves come off at the various levels of the spinal cord, although there is some overlapping of the segments. However, specialised areas such as the limbs take the supplies from more than one segment as they require a more complex supply. In the head this supply is more complex still due to the specialised nature of the area. There are still the basic types of nerve but they come from within the skull and are called cranial nerves. Twelve cranial nerves are recognised, and the important ones in the region in which we are dealing are as follows:

(a) the fifth cranial nerve (V) (trigeminal nerve), which supplies sensation to the face and most of the oral tissues, and supplies the motor function of the muscles of mastication. This nerve is conveniently divided into:

   (i) an ophthalmic division supplying sensation to the skin above the angle of the eye;

   (ii) a maxillary division which supplies the area of skin between the angle of the eye and the angle of the mouth and includes sensation to the palate and the upper teeth; and

   (iii) a mandibular division which supplies sensation to the area below the angle of the mouth, the lower teeth and, via the lingual nerve branch, to the floor of the mouth and anterior aspect of the tongue. It is from this division that the inferior dental nerve arises which has been mentioned earlier in connection with the anatomy of the mandible;

(b) the seventh cranial nerve (VII) (facial nerve), which supplies the motor function of the muscles of facial expression and only a very small sensory function to the ears;

(c) the ninth cranial nerve (IX) (glossopharyngeal nerve), which supplies sensation to the posterior part of the tongue and has some motor function in the pharynx, the first part of the throat;

(d) the twelfth cranial nerve (XII) (hypoglossal nerve), which supplies the motor function of the tongue itself.

CHAPTER FOUR

DENTAL MORPHOLOGY

ENAMEL

The crowns of all teeth are covered by a white and shiny material called enamel. Though very hard, it is also brittle. It is largely composed of the minerals calcium and phosphorous together with water and proteins, laid down in a crystalline pattern. It has no nerves or blood supply.

DENTINE

Like enamel, dentine is composed of calcium and phosphorous but with a higher proportion of protein (mainly collagen). It provides the bulk of the tooth structure. Dentine is sensitive to a variety of stimuli, eg heat and cold as well as physical damage including that caused by a dental drill.

CEMENTUM

A thin outer covering of the root similar in structure to bone.

PULP

This is contained within the tooth and is made up of connective tissue containing nerve fibres and blood vessels which supply the dentine. The nerve fibres transmit stimuli such as hot and cold from the tooth to the brain, where it is experienced as pain.

PERIODONTIUM – GINGIVAE (GUMS) AND SUPPORTING BONE

The tissue covering the jaw bone around the teeth is called the gingiva or gum. It is firmly bound to the underlying bone and closely adapted to the cervical areas of the teeth. The width of the gingivae varies, with the upper anterior teeth possessing the greatest amount, decreasing posteriorly towards the molars.

Healthy gingivae show knife-edged extensions (papillae) between each tooth and are pink and stippled. Each tooth sits in an individual socket within the jaws. The roots are attached to the bone by distinctive fibres. These fibres run obliquely from the cementum layer to the outermost layer of the bony socket wall. The periodontium also contains numerous blood vessels and nerve fibres. The sling effect of this 'ligament' allows the tooth a certain amount of movement during function. Masticatory (chewing) forces are dissipated by the periodontal ligament, similar in action to the suspension system on a car.

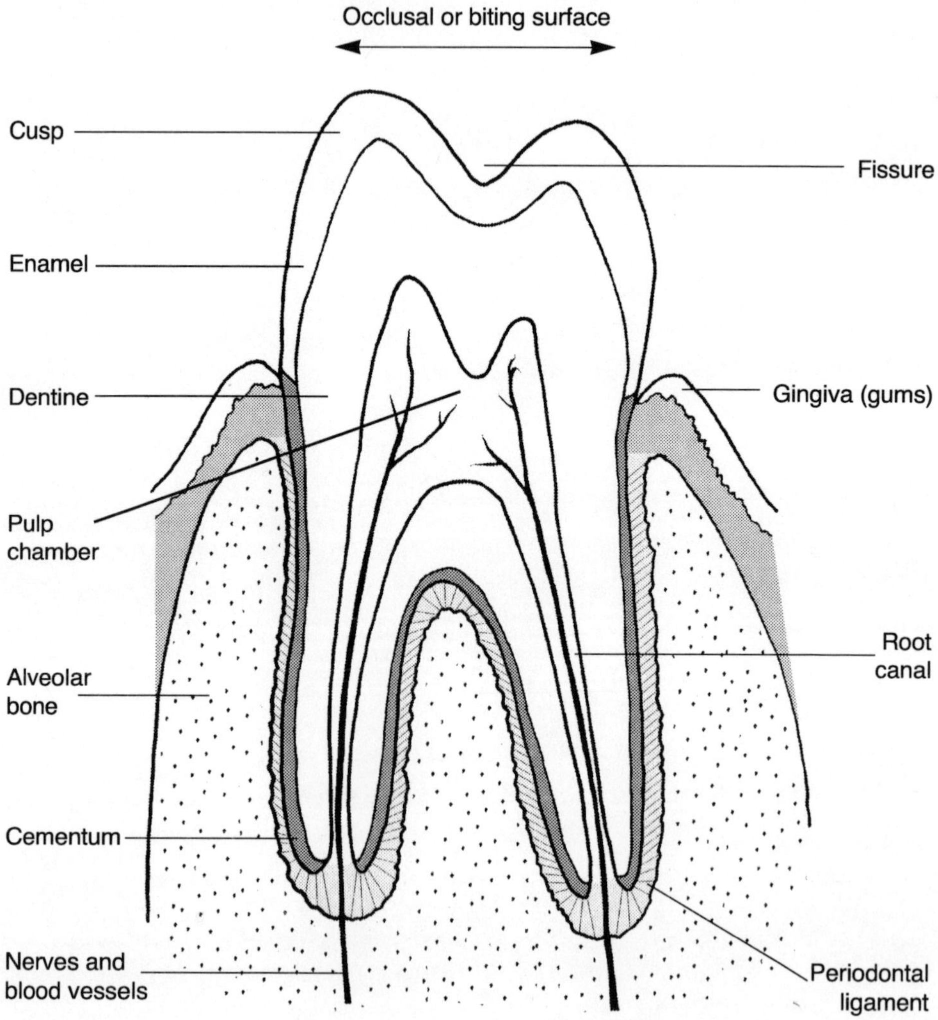

Figure 9. Cross-section through a lower molar tooth.

TYPES OF TEETH

Incisors

These are situated in the front of the mouth in each jaw. The typical crown is shovel shaped and they are single rooted. There are four incisors, two central and two lateral, in each dental arch. In a small percentage of the population the upper lateral incisors are congenitally missing.

Canines

These often have a large crown and are single rooted. There is one canine in each quadrant immediately behind the lateral incisor. They form an important landmark between the anterior and posterior teeth.

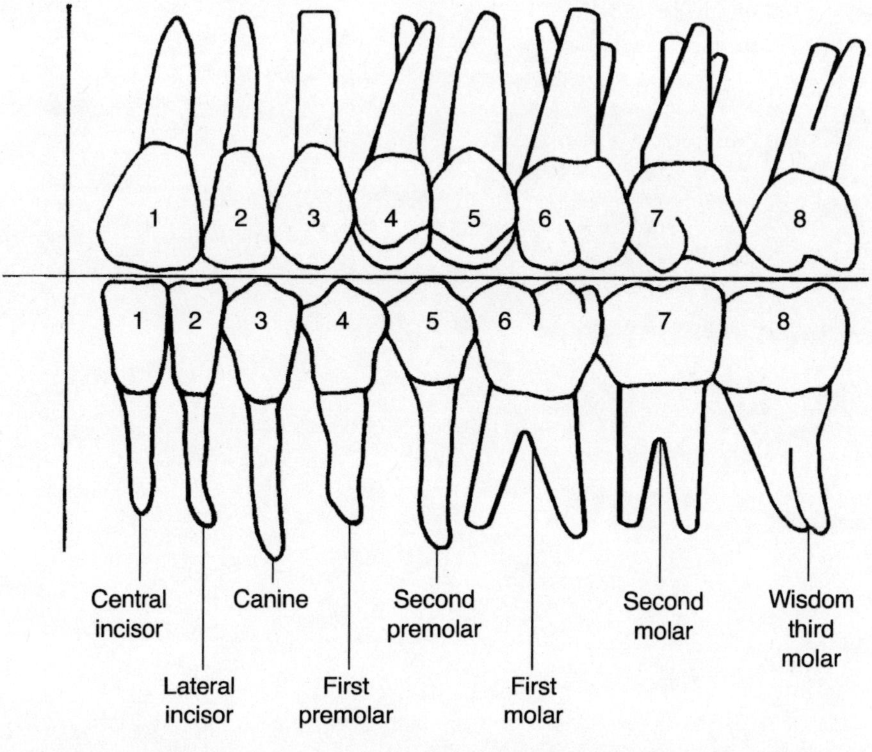

Figure 10. The upper and lower permanent teeth.

Premolars

These can be divided into first and second premolars. The upper first premolar usually has two roots, while the second premolars usually have one. They are also known as bicuspids as they have two cusps, one buccal and one palatal. The lowers are single rooted and smaller than their upper equivalents.

Permanent molars

Upper

These can be divided into first, second and third molars. The upper first and second molars usually possess three roots with three root canals. The occlusal or biting surface of these teeth have a much larger surface area than their preceding premolars. The upper third molars (wisdom teeth) often fail to erupt fully and may possess a more complex root structure.

Lower

As in the upper arch there are first, second and third molars, one in each quadrant. The first and second molars have two roots. The third molars (wisdom teeth) may be absent, unerupted or partially erupted. The root pattern may be simple or complex.

A full set of teeth totals 32, with 16 in each jaw, eight on each side of the mid-line.

Deciduous (milk/baby) teeth

There are 10 in each jaw with five on each side of the mid-line. The crowns are somewhat smaller than their permanent successors and possess large pulp (nerve) chambers. The roots of the molar teeth are shorter and more divergent than in adult teeth, allowing the crowns of the developing premolar teeth to form, safely encircled by them.

ERUPTION TIMES

The deciduous teeth start to develop *in utero*. They erupt into the oral cavity around six months post-natally. The central incisors are the first teeth to erupt, closely followed by the lateral incisors. The first deciduous molars erupt at around 12 months, followed by the canines at 18 months and the second molars at 24 months. There should be a complete deciduous dentition by the age of 30 months.

In respect of the permanent teeth, development starts around birth. Eruption times vary considerably from individual to individual and the average ages are as follows:

(a) first molars 6–7 years;

(b) lower central incisors 6–7 years, upper central incisors 7–8 years;

(c) lateral incisors 7–9 years;

(d) lower canines 9–10 years, upper canines 11–12 years;

(e) upper and lower first premolars 10–11 years;

(f) upper and lower second premolars 11–13 years;

(g) second molars 12–13 years; and

(h) third molars 18–22 years.

The roots of the deciduous teeth are resorbed by the underlying permanent successors leading to loosening and eventual exfoliation of the deciduous dentition. The permanent molars erupt behind the deciduous dentition and therefore do not have a deciduous predecessor. The deciduous molars are replaced by the permanent premolars. Between the ages of 8–13 a great deal of dental development is taking place with the exfoliation of the deciduous teeth, development and eruption of the permanent teeth. This is known as the mixed dentition stage and coincides with an increase in the size of the face.

SURFACES OF THE TEETH

The biting surface of molars and premolars is known as the occlusal surface. The occlusal surface can be divided up into a number of cusps by fissures and pits of varying depth and complexity. The term used for the outer surface of molars and premolars (ie the sides facing the cheeks) is the buccal surface. The outer surface of canines and incisors, which faces the lips, is the labial or buccal surface. All the lower teeth possess surfaces facing the tongue called the lingual surfaces. With upper teeth the surfaces facing the palate are called palatal. Other surfaces of the teeth can be described as follows:

(a) mesial surface – the surface of a tooth which faces towards the front of the mouth; and

(b) distal surface – the surface which faces the back of the mouth.

The descriptive terminology relating to the various surfaces is important when describing the sites of decay and the relevant restorations.

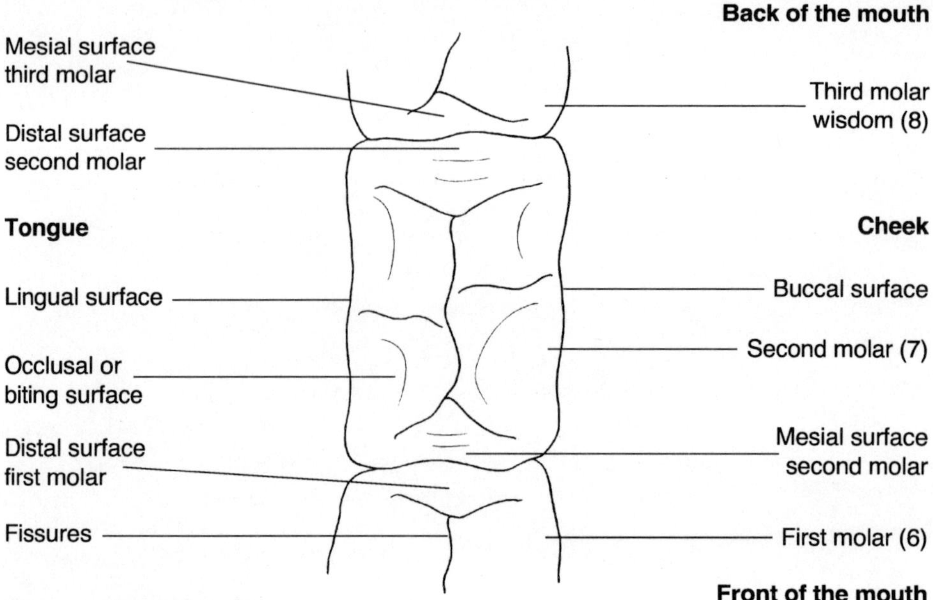

Figure 11. A bird's eye view of the lower molars (occlusal).

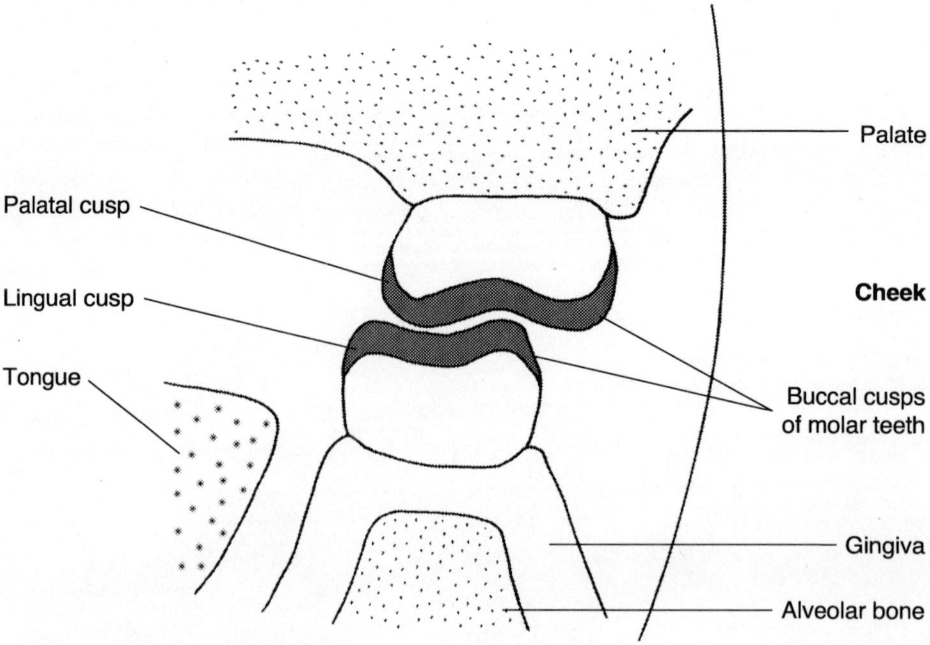

Figure 12. Interdigitation of the teeth (occlusion).

OCCLUSION

When a full upper and lower set of teeth close together and interdigitate with each other, the teeth are said to be 'in occlusion'. The occlusion can vary greatly and depends on a number of factors such as:

(a) loss of deciduous teeth due to decay at an early age, resulting in early eruption of the permanent successors in a more forward or mesial position than normal. This reduces the space for other permanent teeth;

(b) early loss of permanent teeth, eg the first molars, normally due to decay, leading to forward or mesial movement of the second and third molars, often rotating and tilting;

(c) congenital absence of certain teeth, eg upper lateral incisors, second premolars and canines. Upper canines are often absent due to their long path of eruption, as they develop high up in the bone and therefore often become displaced or fail to erupt into their correct position in the dental arch;

(d) supernumerary teeth (additional teeth with abnormal shape) which interfere with the path of eruption of the permanent teeth and, if found, are more likely to be located in the mid-line between the upper central incisors; and

(e) supplemental teeth (addition teeth with normal shape).

The occlusion can be sub-divided, or classified, according to a number of factors which will be discussed in the chapter on orthodontics.

CHAPTER FIVE

DENTAL CHARTING

CHARTING

Each tooth, whether deciduous or permanent, has an individual letter or number to identify it. The dental chart also shows all the tooth surfaces by means of various symbols. Disease and treatment to these surfaces can be recorded as follows:

(a) teeth present or missing;

(b) teeth requiring extraction or recently removed;

(c) surfaces restored (filled);

(d) surfaces that require restoring;

(e) more complex restorations, eg crown and bridge work, implants and dental prostheses (dentures);

(f) gum problems;

(g) root fillings.

The upper and lower dental arches are split into four quadrants and denoted as follows:

(a) upper right ┘

(b) upper left └

(c) lower right ┐

(d) lower left ┌

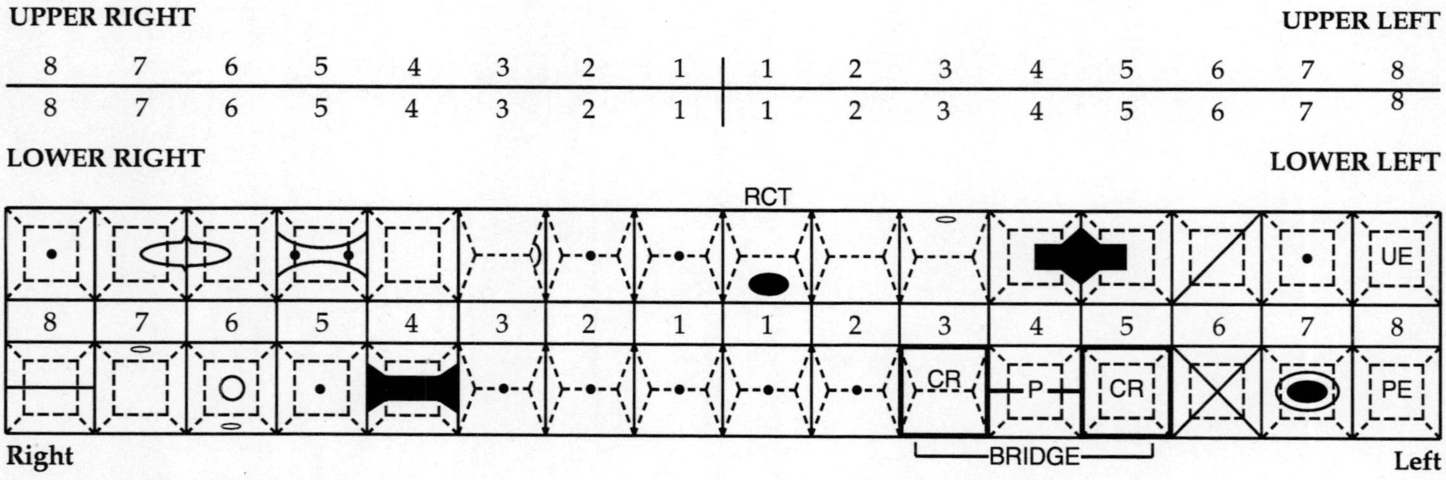

7⌋	Mesio/occlusal cavity (MO)
6⌋	Disto/occlusal cavity (DO)
5⌋	Mesio/occ/distal cavity (MOD)
7⌉	Lingual cavity
6⌉	Occlusal and buccal cavities
3⌋	Mesial cavity
8⌉	Missing
4⌉	MOD restoration
1⌋	Palatal restoration and root canal treatment
⌊3	Labial or buccal cavity
⌊4	DO restoration
⌊5	MO restoration
⌊6	To be extracted
⌈8	Partially erupted
⌊8	Unerupted
⌈7	Occlusal restoration in need of refilling
⌈6	Recently extracted
⌈3+5	Bridge
⌈35	Abutments for crowns

Figure 13. A dental chart.

DENTAL CHART

If the upper left hand quadrant is used as an example, the teeth are notated as follows:

|1 central incisor

|2 lateral incisor

|3 canine

|4 first premolar

|5 second premolar

|6 first molar

|7 second molar

|8 third molar

Similar numbers are given to each tooth in the other three quadrants.

With the deciduous teeth the quadrant system still applies, but each tooth is given a letter:

|A central incisor

|B lateral incisor

|C canine

|D first molar

|E second molar

This dental notation is the best known and most widely used in the UK. All the National Health Service charts use it, and therefore all practitioners in Britain are conversant with the system.

The International Dental Federation (FDI) uses a different numbering system, and it is this which is most commonly used in the USA. In time, we believe this international system may be adopted by all countries in order to present a uniform charting system which can be understood by dental surgeons the world over.

Again the teeth are split into four quadrants and a separate number given to each tooth, as shown below:

18 17 16 15 14 13 12 11	21 22 23 24 25 26 27 28
48 47 46 45 44 43 42 41	31 32 33 34 35 36 37 38

Deciduous teeth are also described in a similar way:

55 54 53 52 51	61 62 63 64 65
85 84 83 82 81	71 72 73 74 75

PERIODONTAL CHARTING

The periodontal status of a patient can be visualised on a chart built up from information taken from all the diseased areas. This involves recording all the dental anomalies and the depth of any pockets around each tooth, and transferring this information onto the chart. The extent of the periodontal destruction can then be assessed for future treatment planning. Pocket depths and areas of recession are measured using a standard measuring probe. Together with radiographic (X-ray) evidence a complex map relating to the periodontal status of the patient can be constructed. (See Figure 14 on page 31.)

A periodontal charting system called CPITN (Community Periodontal Index of Treatment Needs), has been developed for use when carrying out epidemiological surveys. It is quick to undertake and therefore large populations can be assessed. Information is obtained which provides some idea of the patients periodontal status at the time of examination.

The CPITN is accepted by the World Health Organisation and the FDI. It has now been recommended for use in general dental practice.

CPITN SYSTEM

A periodontal probe with a 0.5mm ball end is used. It is marked with bands to show distances from the tip so that pocket depths can be recorded. The mouth is split up into sextants and a single score from the worst tooth in each sextant is used and recorded on a chart.

3	1	3
4	0	3

Code:
- 0 – Healthy periodontium
- 1 – bleeding after probing
- 2 – calculus (tartar) present around defective margins of fillings or crowns
- 3 – up to 5.5mm pocketing
- 4 – >6mm depth of pocketing

The highest code (ie the worst result) found on any tooth in the sextant is recorded in one of the boxes. Each patient is then managed with respect to the scoring attained. This will range from simple oral hygiene instruction and scaling to more complex treatments such as surgery, though scores of 3 and 4 will require further examination and charting before progressing to treatment.

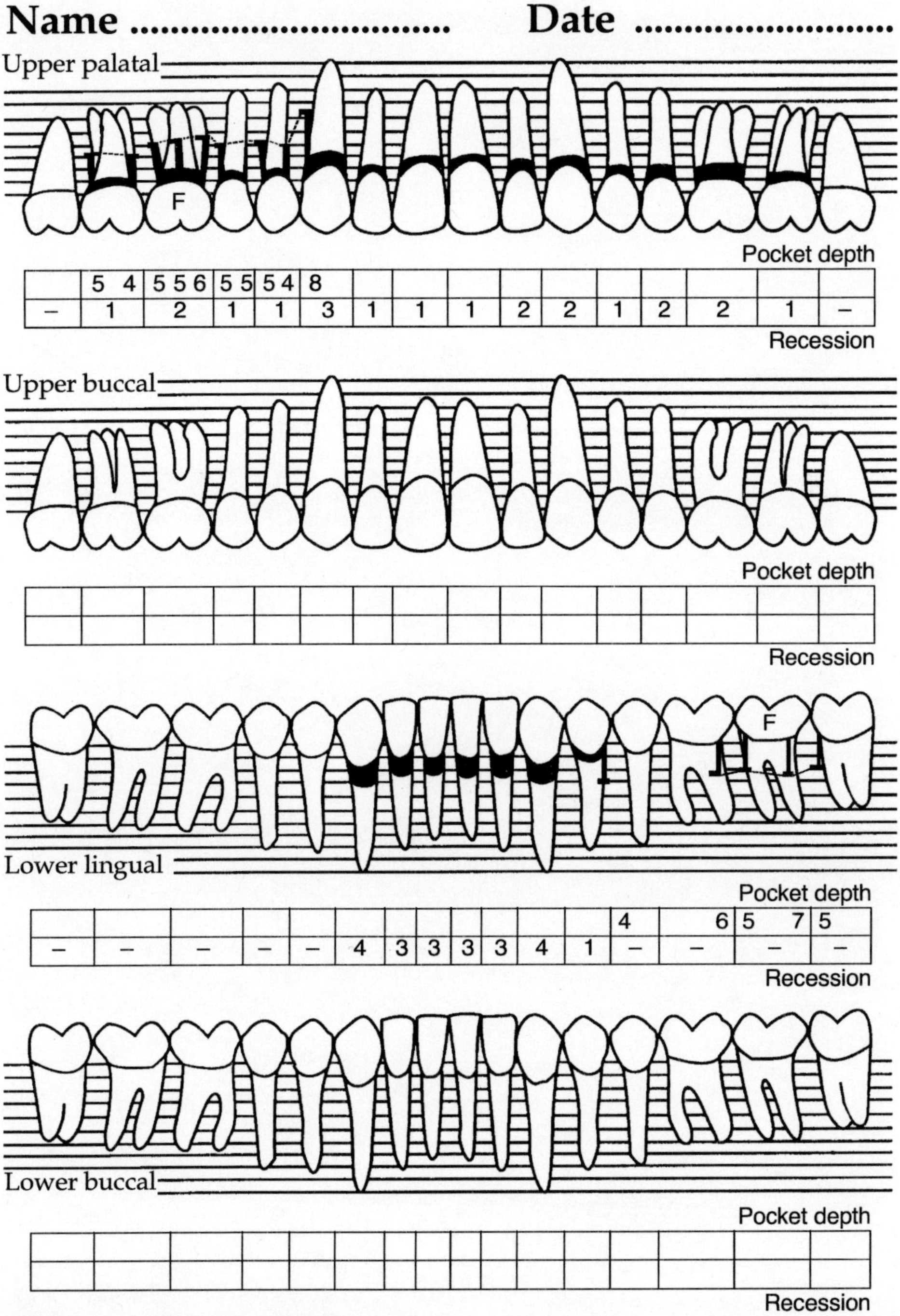

Figure 14. A periodontal chart.
F (furcation) = pocket extending into the region between the roots.

CHAPTER SIX

DISEASE PROCESSES

The study of disease is called pathology. In simple terms this is the scientific study of the way in which things go wrong and their effects on the various organs of the body. This chapter will describe in outline what these processes are. All these pathological problems may occur in the mouth and may be referred to in later chapters.

The body is maintained in a state of health by the many adjustments which homeostatic mechanisms in the body make every second. Failure of any of these systems can lead to disease processes. This failure may take a number of simple forms. It may be a failure of a control system or an inability to respond to an insult such as an infection, or the response itself may be adequate but may turn against the host instead of the cause of the original imbalance. Broadly, the processes which give rise to problems can be listed as: neoplasia; degeneration; inflammation; and congenital and inherited diseases.

NEOPLASIA

Neoplasia means new growth. It is an area of tissue whose normal growth regulation has been affected, resulting in uncontrolled growth independent of its parent tissue. The word 'tumour' simply means a lump, although it is often used synonymously with neoplasia.

Neoplasia is usually divided into two groups:

(a) benign;

(b) malignant.

A benign neoplasm is composed of tissue which is usually indistinguishable from surrounding normal tissue, has well defined borders, grows slowly and is not usually life-threatening unless interfering with some adjacent important structure. A malignant neoplasm is characterised by being poorly separated from surrounding tissue and consisting of abnormal cells which are fast growing and which exhibit the particular characteristic of infiltration into surrounding tissues in an uncontrolled way. Furthermore, by spreading into the adjacent blood, lymph vessels or body cavities, small parts of a malignant neoplasm may become detached and spread to distant sites of the body (metastasis). It is this latter group of malignant neoplasms which are commonly called 'cancers' after the sign of the Zodiac – Cancer the crab. This is because they are said to appear like a crab with a central 'body' of neoplastic tissue and long thin 'legs' of infiltrating growth.

Almost any tissue in the body is capable of becoming malignant. However, around the oral cavity the vast majority of neoplasms are squamous cell carcinomata which are malignant neoplasms of epithelial cells. Malignant tumours from bone or tooth substance also occur within the jaws themselves, and malignant tumours of blood cells (leukaemias) and lymphoid tissue (lymphomas) often produce signs and symptoms within the area.

A further complication arises since areas of mucosa may show alteration before reaching the state of malignancy. This produces diagnostic difficulties since the presentation of these lesions may be indistinguishable from other totally benign conditions which commonly occur. The clinician is often faced with the dilemma that, although he may be 99% sure that a lesion is benign, he cannot totally rule out the possibility of an early malignant lesion. The treatment of malignant lesions is made vastly easier the earlier they are detected, and the prognosis with a malignant lesion deteriorates rapidly with time. The clinician may often, therefore, opt to remove a sample surgically (biopsy) to be sure of the diagnosis, even though this means a patient may be left with a small scar. This area of practice is one that may give rise to litigation since, on the one hand, patients may undergo surgery for what is initially thought a malignant lesion but later turns out to be benign, on the other hand, a malignant tumour may be missed until it is past the point of successful treatment.

DEGENERATION

This may be defined as the progressive loss of structure and function caused by processes other than neoplasia or inflammation. These are often general changes due to age, poor nutrition, poisons, ionising radiation or lack of use. Description of all these individual conditions is beyond the scope of his book, and except for one or two specific processes, which will be described in subsequent chapters, they only form a very small proportion of disease in the mouth.

INFLAMMATION

Inflammation itself is a specific term. It has four cardinal signs which are:

(a) redness;

(b) heat;

(c) swelling;

(d) pain.

It is the reaction of the body to an injury which may be direct trauma, excessive heat or cold, irritant chemicals, ionising radiation or attack by microbiological agents. In the mouth, the commonest causes of inflammation are trauma, due to either direct physical injury or burning from hot foods or liquids, and infection, which may or may not lead to abscess formation.

Inflammation may be considered acute or chronic. Acute inflammation is the reaction of the local micro-circulation to the insult. There is an outflowing of cells and fluid from damaged or reacting vessels. This being necessary to bring specialised defensive cells and chemicals to the area, both to ward off potential attack by invading micro-organisms and to deal with other chemical substances and initiate repair processes. It is this that causes the redness, the swelling, the increase in temperature and, via various chemicals acting on nerve ends, initiates pain.

Chronic inflammation is a more prolonged state in which attempted repair by the body is frustrated by continuation of the process causing the initial damage.

The whole process of inflammation is initially local to the area involved, depending on the severity of the initial insult the efficacy of the body's response and attempts to keep it contained. However, the process may or may not spread to involve the whole body. It is necessary at this point to go into a little more detail about infective causes of inflammation.

Infection by micro-organisms is an important and common cause of inflammation. Many micro-organisms, however, exist quite happily in the body. Some live simply as commensals (living harmlessly with each other) and others have a more symbiotic relationship with beneficial effects to the host. Other micro-organisms may invade and cause disease, although it is important to realise that almost any micro-organism under the right condition may cause disease, and indeed some of the most severe illnesses may be caused by bacteria which, although normally commensal in the body, under certain circumstances may become the cause of serious illness. Specific examples of these will be dealt with later in the chapter. There are a variety of micro-organisms which cause infections in man and these will be briefly described.

BACTERIA

These are well organised and have the innate ability not only to survive but to reproduce. Many can survive in a resting form in unfavourable conditions, therefore surviving outside the body. They may lie in this resting state for extremely long periods of time. Bacteria are traditionally classified depending on their shape, eg round (termed cocci) or elongated (termed bacilli, etc), and on their ability to retain a stain called the 'gram stain' therefore belonging to gram-positive or gram-negative groups.

VIRUSES

These are very small organisms normally only seen via high power (electron) microscopy. They are composed of the genetic information necessary for replication but can only multiply using the 'equipment' found within animal or plant cells. They may also survive for long periods outside of the body, although equally many are much more fragile and are readily destroyed when out of their natural environment.

There are some micro-organisms (*Rickettsiae* and *Mycoplasmae*) which do not fall into the category of viruses or bacteria but have some features of both.

PROTOZOA

These are more highly organised than bacteria but still consist of only one cell. A typical example is the amoeba; however, this group of micro organisms rarely cause problems within the mouth.

FUNGI

These are more complex organisms and usually fall within the plant kingdom. They produce branching extensions to their cells and are a common cause of oral infection due to their ubiquitous nature, eg oral thrush (candidosis).

HELMINTHS

These are worms and, although they are a very important cause of disease, particularly in third world countries, they do not form an important cause of oral disease in this country.

CONGENITAL AND INHERITED DISEASES

These two terms are not synonymous. A congenital disease is one with which a person is born, whereas an inherited disease is caused by the genetic pattern inherited from one's parents. An example is cleft palate which, although always congenital, may or may not be inherited.

This area is a complex one. It includes infections, eg syphilis, which may be contracted whilst in the womb and would therefore be congenital. It also encompasses obvious malformations in structure, diseases which may only manifest themselves at a later date, and even more subtle changes in susceptibility to conditions to which a person may or may not be subjected later in life. Anatomical deformities may arise as single isolated phenomena or may be part of a more generalised groups of problems as part of a specific syndrome.

NECROSIS

The term necrosis in pathology is not synonymous with the word death. It is used to describe particular pathological processes that take place in the cell when the latter is damaged, to the extent that it ceases to function as a normal cell and undergoes various degenerative changes from which it cannot recover. A cell may cease to function normally without undergoing necrosis.

SYNDROME

The term syndrome is one which is often used in medicine, and describes a collection of signs and symptoms which occur together in the same patient for reasons other than random misfortune. It is important to realise that not all individual signs or symptoms may be present in each case, and that the severity of a syndrome may vary widely from one patient to another, eg Down's syndrome

Down's syndrome is a condition with a well recognised group of signs. It is a result of the presence in an individual of three chromosomes number 21 instead of the usual two.

Its features include mental retardation and physical signs such as short stature, small head, mongoloid slant of the eyes, epicanthic fold in the eyelid, large fissured tongue and rough skin. There may be heart defects, gastrointestinal defects and various other organ system defects.

VIRULENCE AND RESISTANCE

Virulence is a term used to describe the pathogenicity of a micro-organism. It is a complex measurement depending on the ability of the organism to multiply, invade the host tissues, overcome defence systems and to cause damage to host.

The resistance of the host encompasses all its standing defence systems and its ability to adapt and develop further methods of preventing damage by the invading micro-organism.

Many factors including environmental ones affect these two functions and the balance between the two may vary with time depending on the general state of the host.

Commensal organisms can therefore become pathogenic when conditions favour this and a common example in the mouth is candidosis. The fungus candida albicans is a commensal organism found in the mouth and normally causes no problems, however, when the resistance of the host is lowered for any reason it may increase rapidly in growth, invade the mucosa and cause a number of conditions the commonest of which is 'thrush'.

CHAPTER SEVEN

DENTAL DISEASES

DENTAL CARIES

This is the process that leads to dental cavities. For many years it has been known that micro-organisms are essential in the pathogenesis of dental caries. Micro-organisms are found in vast numbers in saliva and plaque. Plaque is a soft, sticky material found on tooth surfaces which is not easily removed by rinsing. It gives rise to a 'furry' feel to the teeth when felt by the tongue. After the teeth have been thoroughly cleaned with a toothbrush a thin layer, the pellicle, quickly forms on the clean tooth surface. This is virtually free of bacteria and is probably derived from salivary proteins. This 'skin' is quickly covered by masses of micro-organisms to form the plaque. Later, as the plaque gets older, other micro-organisms appear to take up residence in the plaque to build up a layered structure.

Plaque thickens on tooth surfaces through the adherence of further organisms and by way of micro-organisms proliferating in the plaque. A matrix is formed in the plaque which becomes abundant when sugars such as sucrose are being consumed in large amounts. Sucrose, as well as other types of sugars, are metabolised (processed) by the micro-organisms in the plaque into other, more complex, sugars (polysaccharides) which helps to increase the volume of the plaque matrix. With consumption of a sugary solution there is a substantial increase in acidity within the plaque. When this acidity reaches a certain level the tooth surface begins to break down (demineralise).

There is now a great deal of evidence that certain bacteria (*Streptococci* species) can give rise to caries, especially if a diet containing high concentrations of carbohydrates such as sucrose are ingested. Other types of organism may also be involved in the carious process, and it is interesting to note that the bacterial flora present when caries has progressed into the dentine substance of the tooth differs considerably from the flora on the surface of the enamel.

With demineralisation of the enamel and dentine a cavity is formed. In the deepest part of the cavity, the advancing front of bacteria slowly breaks down the mineralised tissues extending the depth of the cavity which, after a period of time, contaminates the pulp chamber of the tooth. The pulp chamber will eventually become infected with bacteria and an inflammatory response occurs leading to the death of the tooth. Necrosis of the tissues within the pulp chamber and root canals occurs and eventually leads to abscess formation in the surrounding bone.

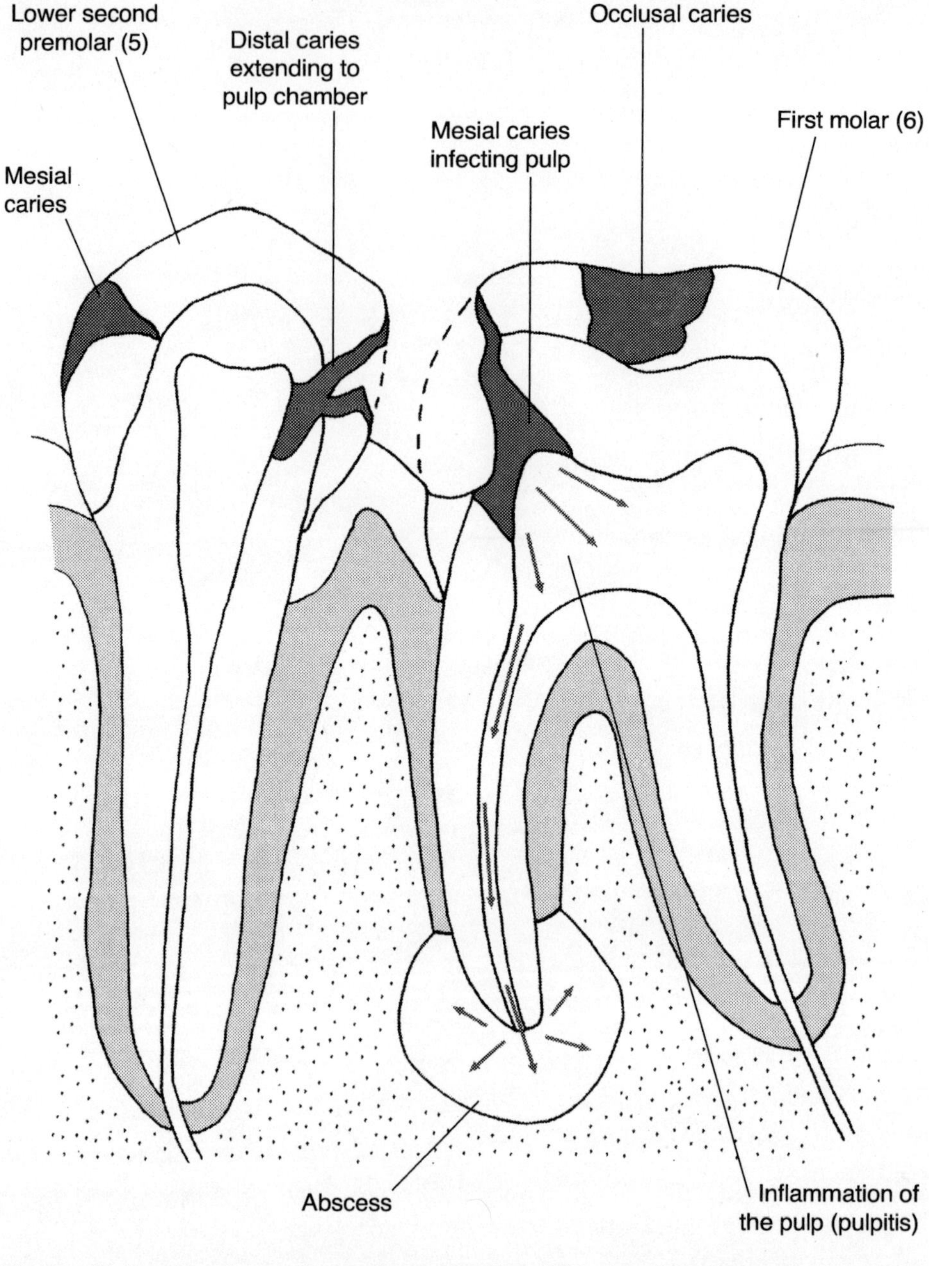

Figure 15. Section through two lower teeth with extensive decay.

A dental abscess usually occurs at the apex of a tooth within the supporting bone and, if acute in nature, will give rise to severe pain, swelling, malaise and pyrexia (increase in body temperature). The tooth will be very tender to bite on and may also become loose and extruded from its socket. The infection results in pus being formed which requires draining. This can be achieved by either:

(a) removing the tooth;

(b) drilling a cavity in the crown of the tooth in order to expose the nerve chamber and root canal; or

(c) incision and drainage of the swelling at the most dependent point.

The severity of dental abscesses depends on a number of important factors:

(a) the host resistance to the organism or organisms involved;

(b) the virulence of the organism; and

(c) systemic factors, eg coexisting medical problems such as diabetes, malignant disease, HIV infection and drugs, all of which reduce host resistance.

The expanding dental abscess follows the path of least resistance in the bone, and therefore may well discharge through the buccal plate (external wall) of bone into the overlying tissues and eventually into the oral cavity or onto the face. A communication between the abscess and the oral cavity or face is known as a sinus and, when the abscess is discharging through this communication, the swelling often reduces and the symptoms are relieved.

The abscess now changes from an acute infection to that of a chronic one. The source of infection at the end of the root is still present but, because a route for discharge exists, little or no symptoms are apparent. The diseased area of the bone surrounding the tooth is, however, still progressing at a slow rate.

With the advent of antibiotics just after the Second World War, the morbidity of dental abscesses greatly lessened, although on occasions, even today, patients have to be admitted to hospital for surgical drainage of dental abscesses which have not responded to the usual treatment of extraction, drainage through the tooth, and antibiotics.

PERIODONTAL DISEASE

Healthy periodontal tissues

The necks of the teeth are surrounded by gingivae (gums) which in health are pink, firm and stippled. Between the gingivae and the tooth is a potential sulcus, at the base of which the gingivae attach to the tooth by a specialised connection known as the epithelial attachment. Below this attachment are fibres which support the tooth in the socket (periodontal ligament).

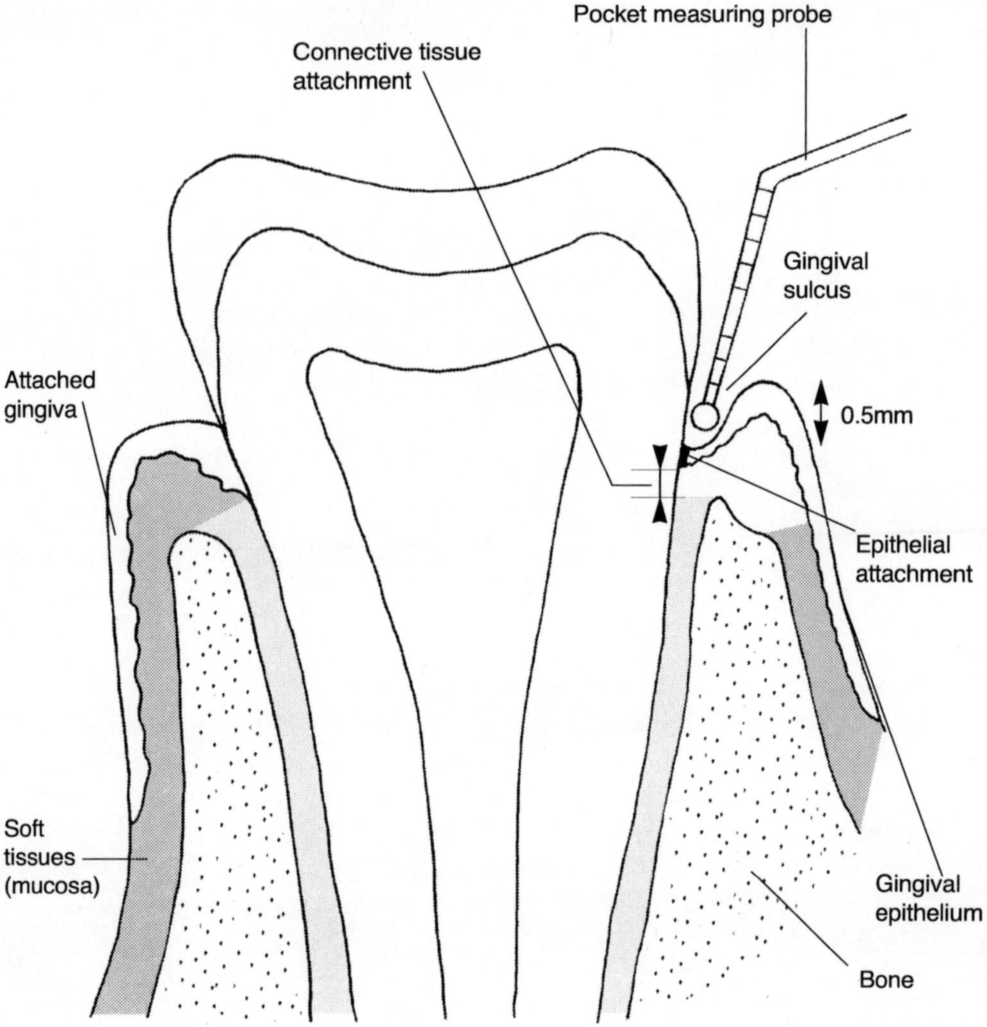

Figure 16. Healthy periodontal tissues; no loss of connective tissue attachment.

Chronic periodontitis

Periodontal disease is generally regarded as a slow, progressive and irreversible disease of the tissues supporting the teeth. If the disease process is not arrested then the affected teeth invariably develop signs of increasing mobility or looseness and therefore require extraction. Periodontal or gum abscesses may also occur and, like dental abscesses, can lead to severe pain, swelling, pus formation and increased mobility which may eventually lead to extractions as well. The main aetiological factors in the progression of periodontal disease is the presence of bacterial plaque. Before our present knowledge concerning bacterial plaque, the term 'getting long in the tooth' was considered to be a natural consequence of increasing age rather than a disease process.

The course of the disease may progress over many years and will, in most cases, remain painless unless an acute abscess develops. In the early stages of the disease process, gingivitis (inflammation of the gums) becomes apparent. The gums lose their pink stippled appearance, become red, smooth, swollen and may exhibit spontaneous bleeding.

The response of the individual to dental plaque is inflammation of the gingivae. The severity of the inflammatory response may well be dependent on the content of the plaque, the duration of the presence of plaque and the response of the host or individual.

This response is variable from person to person, as some individuals may develop very rapid breakdown of the supporting bone and therefore may well lose a number of teeth much earlier in life, compared to other individuals where the disease process may be much slower and less destructive.

The type of organisms present in the plaque and their specific role in the disease process is complex but appears to involve the hosts immunological system, ie the body's defences. Inflammation of the gingiva, given time, progresses to periodontitis and the gingivae become detached from the necks of the teeth, forming a pocket between the root surface and the gingival wall. As the pocket deepens, the plaque forms further down the root. This area is inaccessible to normal oral hygiene methods. The disease process continues, leading to progressive loss of the periodontal ligament which attaches the root to the socket wall, and also to the loss of the bone surrounding the tooth. The disease process may have periods of remission and destruction which vary in severity from person to person. In the early stages of the disease, ie gingivitis, adequate oral hygiene removes the adherent plaque at the cervical margins of the teeth which will lead to resolution of the inflammation and a return to gingival health.

Other factors may well modify the disease process and these can be split up into extrinsic and intrinsic factors.

(a) Extrinsic – local conditions in and around the dental arches which exacerbate the accumulation of plaque. These include poor contact areas between teeth, rough surfaces from poorly contoured restorations, prostheses, smoking, and the intake of a soft sugary diet.

(b) Intrinsic (systemic) factors:

   (i) drugs, eg Epanutin, which predispose to proliferation of the gums, which in some cases cover the teeth completely;

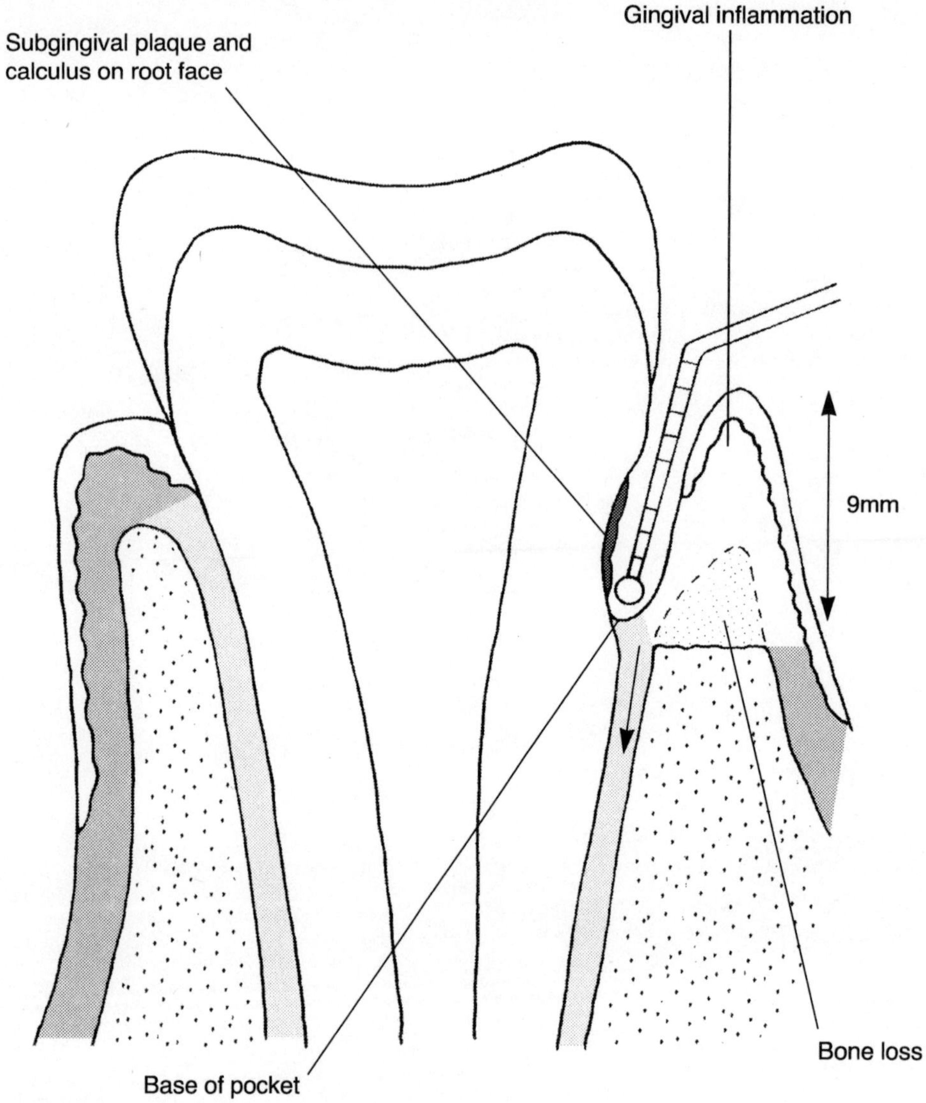

Figure 17. Severely diseased periodontal tissue; loss of connective tissue attachment and pocket formation.

(ii) systemic diseases, eg diabetes, leukaemia and nutritional deficiencies such as lack of vitamin C (still found occasionally in old people living alone on a poor diet);

(iii) genetic anomalies (Down's syndrome); and

(iv) hormonal status, eg pregnancy.

Acute ulcerative gingivitis

A more aggressive gingivitis may occur in some individuals known as acute ulcerative gingivitis (AUG). In the past it used to be referred to as Vincent's infection or trench mouth, since it was extremely common among the troops fighting in the trenches during the First World War. The lack of oral hygiene, inadequate diet as well as a generally lowered disease resistance led to this acute infection becoming rife. This condition is thought to be caused by various organisms acting together and is characterised by the loss of the papillae between the teeth resulting in ulceration, sloughing of the tissues, bleeding, pain and bad breath (halitosis). This condition usually clears up with improved oral hygiene, scaling and improved overall conditions such as diet, hygiene and adequate sleep. When all these conditions are corrected the tissues normally return to a healthy state, although the actual loss of tissue between the teeth (papillae) will not grow back.

Juvenile periodontitis

A severe inflammatory disease which is often diagnosed in the early teens, and more often than not is localised to the incisors and first molar teeth. The bacterial flora involved in this disease process may well be different from the flora involved in chronic periodontitis. It is thought there may be an immunological defect present which produces an inadequate host response to the bacteria and hence rapid destruction.

Gingival recession

This may be caused by traumatic injury due to improper tooth brushing, eg the horizontal sawing action which can be most destructive. This is often seen if certain teeth, eg the upper canines, which are often very prominent and the brush will tend to act heavily on them. Other teeth may also show isolated areas of recession, especially if they have erupted in a more forward position in the arch. These teeth will often have little or no covering of bone or gingivae and therefore any irritation, whether mechanical, thermal or plaque induced, may well lead to a rapid loss of tissue and hence extensive recession. Recession may occur instead of pocket formation during the periodontal disease process, but the reason for this is unknown and open to further research.

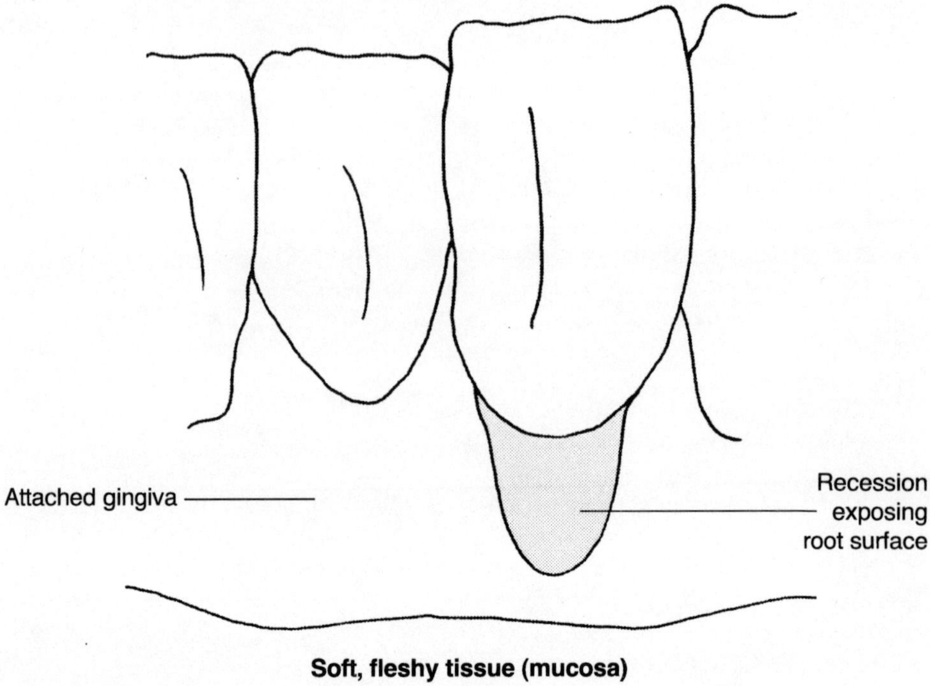

Figure 18. Labial view of lower incisors.

Traumatic gingivitis

The gingivae may well become damaged from direct injury through certain agents such as drugs. The classic Aspirin burn occurs as a result of patients with toothache trying to relieve the discomfort with the insertion of an Aspirin tablet which is allowed to dissolve on the gingivae in the area of the discomfort. In dentistry a number of toxic agents are used in certain procedures and these may well give rise to destruction of the gingival and bony tissues.

Devitalising compounds

These materials are used to kill remaining vital contents of a pulp or nerve chamber prior to carrying out root canal therapy. Some of these agents contain phenol and paraformaldehyde; if left for any length of time around the periodontal tissues, necrosis will occur and localised loss of bone.

CHAPTER EIGHT

ANALGESIA, SEDATION AND ANAESTHESIA

Of all the major advances in dentistry in the past 100 years, the most important has been the relief of pain and the more unpleasant symptoms of stress related to the various procedures undertaken. The development of painkilling drugs, safe anaesthetic agents and various form of sedation have made the business of dentistry more pleasant for both the patient and the dentist.

ANALGESIA

Analgesia means the relief of pain. It may be general, by the use of drugs such as Aspirin and Paracetamol which, when taken, will relieve pain from different causes in various parts of the body, or may be localised, most usually by injection or spraying of a local analgesic agent. Although often termed local anaesthesia, it should more correctly be termed local analgesia since it relieves pain rather than induces sleep.

Local analgesia is the commonest form of pain relief used in dentistry. Various drugs are used, all of which are derivatives of cocaine, which have been developed to produce more pronounced relief of pain without many of the central effects of the parent drug itself. The efficacy of these drugs means there is no longer any place for the use of cocaine in routine dentistry. The commonest drug in use is Lignocaine, with Prilocaine, Lidocaine and Bupivacaine being alternatives sometimes used. Although they may be used on their own, the effect can be enhanced by addition of a drug which constricts local blood vessels and therefore slows removal of the analgesic solution. The most common agent being adrenaline.

Local analgesic solutions are used either as an infiltration around the site of the operation or may be injected around a nerve trunk, thereby preventing a nerve impulse transmission which renders pain-free the area of the body the nerve normally supplies. In dentistry it is usual to use nerve blocks for the lower jaw but infiltrations for the upper jaw. The nerve blocks in the lower jaw are aimed at the inferior dental nerve described earlier, which enters the mandible far back in the mouth and needs to be blocked via a blind technique. Although it is a very safe procedure with many millions completed safely every year, it does occasionally give rise to complications, particularly if direct damage to the nerve occurs.

SEDATION

Sedation means relaxing a patient and removing the unpleasant symptoms associated with anxiety and stress. Many sedative agents also act as analgesics, but not all. The most common methods of sedation are by the use of intravenous drugs, oral drugs, gaseous agents and hypnosis. The intravenous agents are the benzodiazepines, the most commonly used being diazepam (Valium) and midazolam (Hypnovel).

Although many other anaesthetic agents may be used in low doses to produce sedation, the risks of full anaesthesia and other side effects make them unsuitable for use by people not fully trained in anaesthetic procedures. The benzodiazepines have a very good safety record and are used worldwide for sedation. They still need to be used with care and it is important to monitor a patient's general condition throughout. Although, it is accepted that one person may act both to administer the sedation and act as operator, this should only be with a suitably trained assistant to monitor the patient's condition. The report of an expert working party on the use of sedation and anaesthesia in dentistry (Poswillo report)[1] and reports from the General Dental Council, have given clear guidelines regarding this.

The same group of drugs may be used in an oral form given an hour or so before surgery, and many people regard this as an equally effective form of sedation. Benzodiazepines affect the central nervous system and patients should be warned not to drive or operate machinery for a minimum of 24 hours following a procedure during which these drugs are used. The inhaled agent most commonly used for sedation is nitrous oxide. The use of this is termed relative analgesia and the effects are the same as when it is used in ambulances or obstetrics for relief of pain. Nitrous oxide is an anaesthetic agent and will induce sleep in high dose, and machines designed for use with relative analgesia have a safety mechanism so that the percentage of nitrous oxide does not rise above 50%. Only designated machines should be used for relative analgesia.

The techniques of hypnosis and acupuncture are not as widely used and are not successful for all patients. However, in those susceptible they are highly effective and in skilled hands are very safe.

ANAESTHESIA

Local anaesthesia has already been mentioned. General anaesthesia is used less often in dentistry than it was and fewer dentists practice it themselves.

1 *General Anaesthesia, Sedation and Resuscitation in Dentistry: Report of a Working Party*, Poswillo DE, Chairman of the Standing Dental Advisory Committee; HMSO, 1990.

There are now clear guidelines which outlaw the single operator anaesthetist, and the majority of practices now using this technique will have a trained anaesthetist to give the anaesthetics for them. Patients undergoing general anaesthesia, like those having intravenous sedation, have their reactions impaired for some time afterwards, and in both cases they are warned not to drive or operate machinery and must be accompanied home by a responsible adult only when they are recovered sufficiently to do so safely. The use of general anaesthetics is a safe procedure although there is a recognised mortality associated with the procedure, even in young fit people under the best conditions.

CHAPTER NINE

X-RAYS AND PHOTOGRAPHY

X-RAYS

When X-rays strike tissue, some will pass through and can then be detected on the other side on an X-ray film in the same way in which an ordinary light camera catches light rays. The density and quantity of the tissue, through which the X-radiation passes, determines the amount of radiation that is transmitted and therefore gives differing exposure of the film accordingly.

The resulting radiograph, unlike the photograph from a light camera which shows surface detail, gives a shadow of the structures through which the X-rays have passed. The X-rays which are not transmitted through the tissues will either be scattered by them and come out at different angles or may be absorbed. When X-rays are absorbed they may do damage, depending on their energy and on the total amount given. It is this aspect which is used therapeutically when both X-rays and other forms of radiation are used to destroy malignant tissue in the field of radiotherapy. The damage effects of radiation are cumulative and even the relatively low energy X-rays used in diagnostic radiation may be harmful if the patient is exposed to a sufficient dose. The public and staff working with X-ray units must therefore be protected, and the doses used for patients must be kept as low as possible.

X-rays may be measured in various ways. The amount of energy absorbed by a tissue, ie that amount of ionising radiation which causes biological damage, is termed the dose and is a more relevant measure than the exposure. The unit used is the gray (Gy), where 1Gy = 1 joule/kilogram (joule is a measure of energy and kilogram of mass). This replaces an older unit, the rad (1Gy = 100 rads).

Since different types of radiation have different effects for the same absorbed dose a further unit, the sievert (Sv) is used to measure dose equivalence so that different types of radiation may be compared. In practical terms however, when talking about the type of X-rays used in dentistry 1Sv is equivalent to 1Gy.

PROCESSING

After exposure, the X-ray film has to be processed in order to produce the final radiograph. The X-ray film consists of an emulsion of silver bromide which absorbs the X-ray's energy resulting in the formation of crystals of silver. After development, these grains appear black and are fixed chemically to the film. Areas where no crystals form are dissolved in the process and appear clear on the film. Therefore, in general the darker the part of the film the more the X-rays have penetrated and therefore the less dense the tissue over that area has been. Films are always washed to remove the chemicals used in the processing and dried before storage.

RADIATION PROTECTION

It is clearly in the best interests of the patient to have the minimum amount of X-rays consistent with obtaining the information required. In this context however, a negative finding may be as important as a positive one. Unfortunately, since X-rays have the ability, on occasions, to show up unsuspected pathology there is a tendency to use them for blanket investigations. Furthermore, since they provide an accurate record there has been a tendency to use them for this purpose as well.

It is necessary to minimise exposure of the patient as far as possible. The use of good quality, fast film and intensifying screens enables the dose to be reduced, as does correct use of the equipment and good radiographic technique, thus avoiding the necessity of repeating the films. Good processing is also vital.

It has now been agreed that for routine dental X-rays there is no indication to use a lead apron for the patient, and that even pregnant woman are at no increased risk provided the X-ray beam is not directed at the abdomen. However, this is provisional on the use of a good technique with fast film, adequate collimation and good processing. Guidelines are provided by the joint working party of the Nation Radiation Protection Board and the Royal College of Radiologists.

X-rays are produced within a 'controlled area'. Only the patient should be in this controlled area which, for apparatus operating up to 70 kilovolts, is within 1m of the X-ray tube and, for apparatus above this, is 1.5m. It is in the interest of the operator to stand as far away as possible, at least 2m, and all personnel other than the operator should be further away. Even outside this area the operator should not stand in line with the beam.

When large numbers of films are being taken, or films requiring higher doses are used, the controlled area needs to be larger, or it may be necessary to reinforce walls, floors and ceilings with various protective barriers to cut down the radiation dose in adjoining spaces.

Where the workload is above a specified quantity, it is necessary to comply with specific regulations and employ a radiation protection advisor. This advisor is a medical physicist who will give specific advice about protection. The ionising radiation regulations 1985 (SI No 1333), which came into effect in January 1986, derives from the powers given to the Secretary of

State, under the Health and Safety At Work Act 1974. It compels the senior practitioner in each practice to comply with these regulations. These state that the presence of ionising radiation apparatus must be notified to the Health and Safety Executive, and that within the practice a radiation protection supervisor must be appointed. This supervisor, who is a named person, is then responsible for the implementation of the recommendations of the approved code of practice for the *Protection of Persons Against Ionising Radiation Arising from Any Work Activity 1985.*[2] A further 1986 Euratom directive on patient protection emphasises the responsibility of the dental practitioner to be properly trained and to be responsible for all assistants who wish to receive instruction on the technique and of complimentary training with a certificate of competence being issued. The radiation protection supervisor has responsibility to draft and display local rules to ensure compliance with the regulations and code of practice.

TYPES OF X-RAY FILM USED IN DENTISTRY

The commonest type of X-ray used in dentistry is the small intra-oral film used to take pictures of individual areas of the mouth, eg:

(a) bitewings – films showing the crowns of the molar and premolar teeth on one side (Plate 1);

(b) periapicals – small X-rays taken of one or two individual teeth but showing the whole of the tooth including the root (Plate 2);

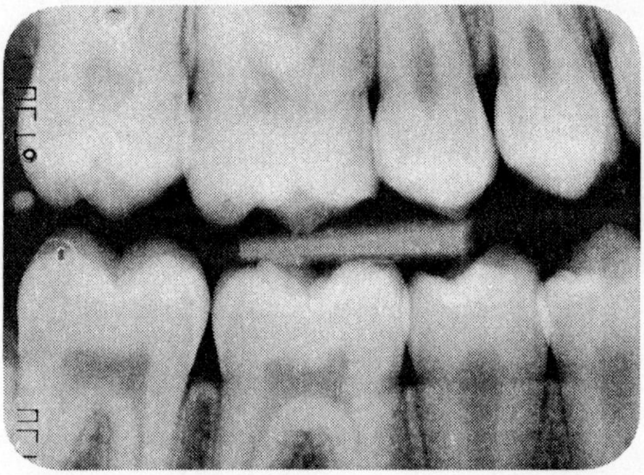

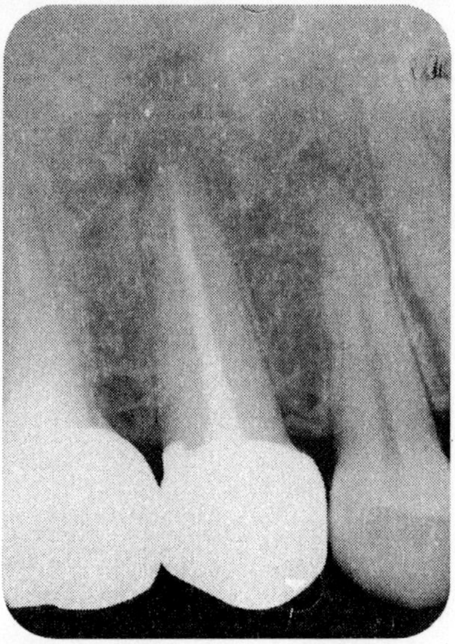

Plate 1, *above,* bitewing radiograph of right upper and lower molar and premolar teeth.
Plate 2, *right,* periapical radiograph of upper right premolars and first molar.
654| or 14, 15, 16.

2 Approved Code of Practice 1985; *The protection of persons against ionising radiation arising from any work activity* – The Ionising Regulations; HMSO, London.

(c) the orthopantomogram (OPG, OPT, Panoral, Panex) – increasingly used in general practice. In this film a continuous picture is taken in the same way that 'long group photographs' used to be taken in schools. The X-ray tube and film rotate around the patient's head in such a way that a narrow slit progresses across the film and exposes each part in turn resulting in a picture of the entire jaw opened out onto the flat surface. Furthermore, this is a tomogram, ie the X-rays are focused in one plane only so that structures in front or behind that plane do not appear clearly on the X-ray (Plate 3).

Occasionally, larger plane films are taken of the jaws although these are mainly used in hospital practice, eg oblique lateral, lateral cephlogram and transpharyngeal view (Plate 4).

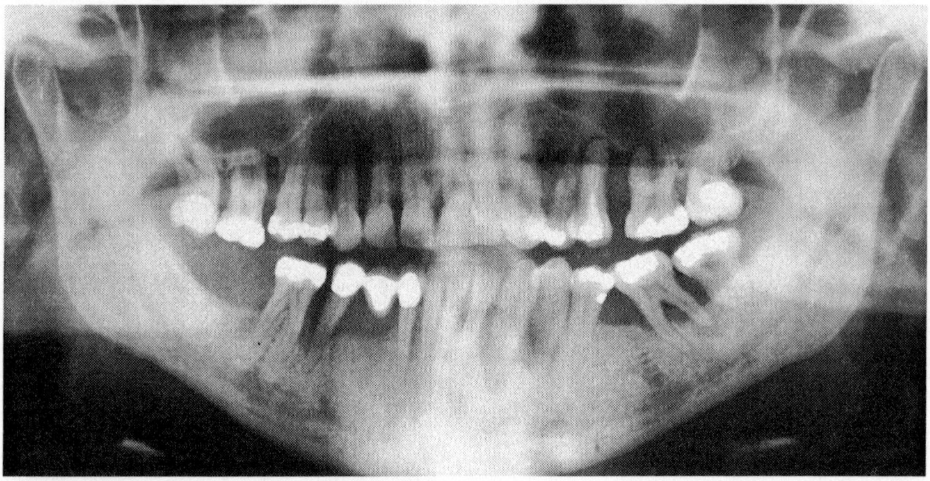

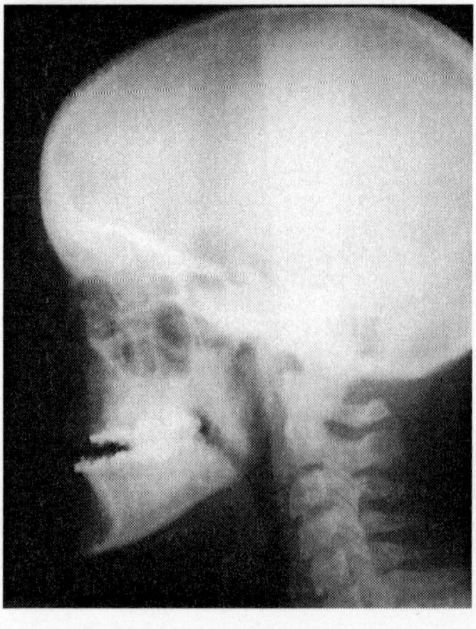

Plate 3, *above,* Orthopantomogram (OPG) showing extensive loss of supporting bone around many teeth due to periodontal disease.

Plate 4, *left,* Lateral Cephalogram. This is a radiograph used to evaluate the jaw positions relative to the rest of the skull. It allows measurements to be made prior to surgery.

COMPUTED TOMOGRAPHY

This type of film is only produced under hospital conditions and consists of multiple exposures in each of several planes through one part of the body. Instead of the X-rays being used to expose a film they are collected by a receiver and turned into an electronic signal which is recorded on magnetic tape. By the use of a computer, these multiple images can be reconstructed to show clear slices through the body or even, if the relevant software is available, build up into three dimensional images (Plates 5; and 6, *overleaf*).

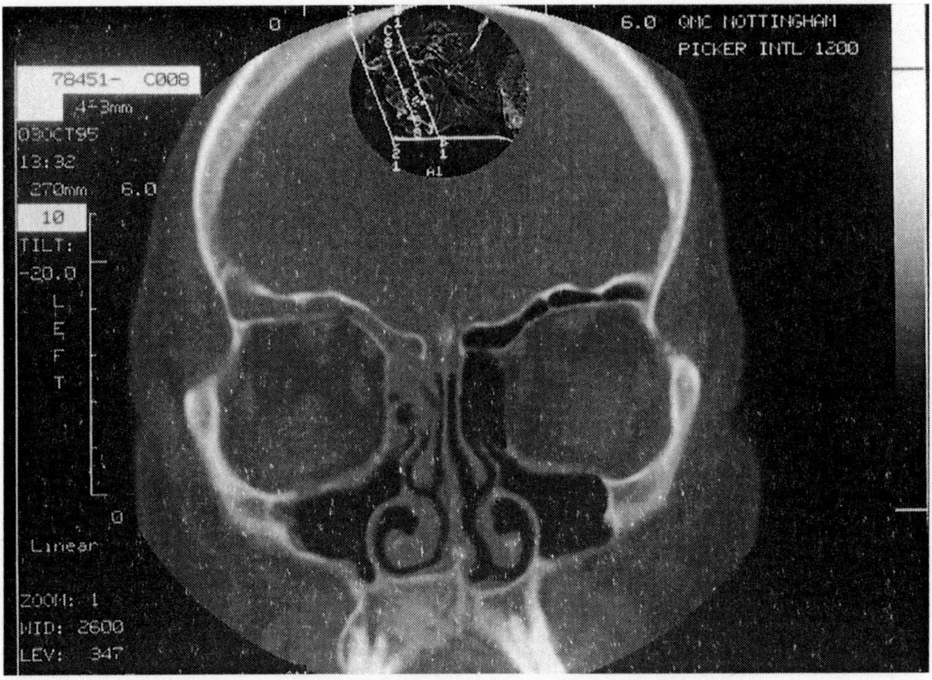

Plate 5, Coronal section of a Computed Tomogram (CT) scan showing a section through the eye sockets, nose and sinuses.

MAGNETIC RESONANCE IMAGING (MRI)

This is a new technology which is now becoming available in hospitals. It involves placing the patient within an extremely powerful magnetic field and then measuring the energy given off from protons within the body as they change position in that field. This does not involve the use of X-rays or any other form of invasive radiation.

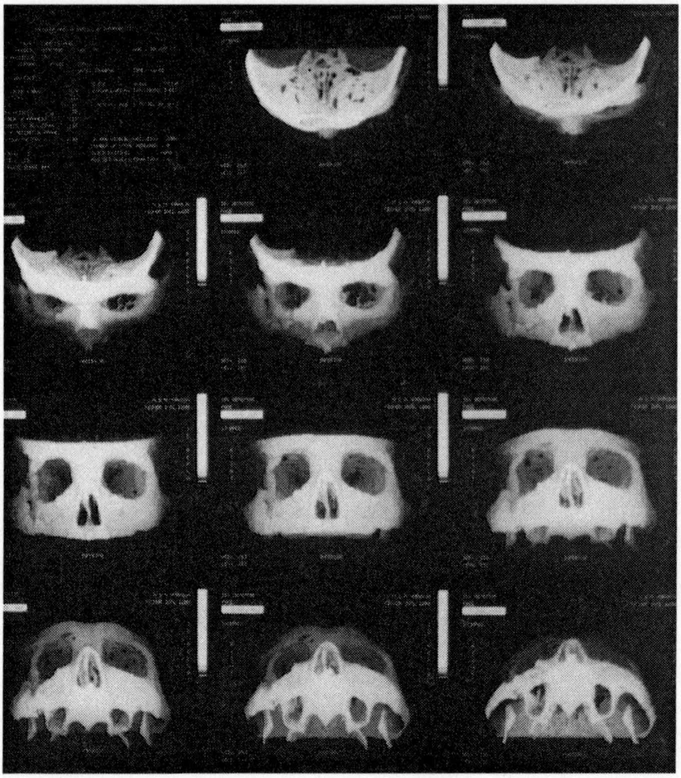

Plate 6, a three dimensional reconstruction from Computed Tomogram (CT) scans showing damage to the right side of the face.

ULTRASOUND

This is an investigative procedure, currently used only in hospitals, which involves the passing of very high frequency sound waves into the tissues and collecting the reflected sound in a similar way that an echo-sounder does on a ship. This is non-invasive although the images are difficult to interpret and require specialist expertise.

PHOTOGRAPHY

The use of extra-oral and intra-oral photography has been increasing in recent years. This has clear advantages from the medico-legal point of view since accurate records are established. Photography is commonly used for three reasons:

(a) as a record to the dentist of the patient's previous condition or interesting pathological conditions;

(b) to produce patient information folders for illustration to other patients of the various facilities and treatments available at the practice; and

(c) for medico-legal reasons.

In general, consent for photography should always be sought, particularly if any publication is envisaged. Many publications will, however, accept photographs where a specific consent is not obtained, provided that the identity of the patient is not apparent. In practical terms this means the eyes need to be blacked out in full facial views. There are currently no legal requirements for dentists to take photographs.

RESTORATIVE DENTISTRY

RESTORATIONS (FILLINGS)

The most common areas for tooth decay to occur are:

(a) The occlusal or biting surfaces of the posterior teeth, notably the premolars and molars, where there are complex pits and fissures; and

(b) inter-proximally where the contact areas between the teeth make access for cleaning difficult.

Treatment of caries

Amalgam has been the material of choice for restoring teeth for well over 100 years. By the mid-1960s white filling materials (silicates) had been introduced which could be used for restoring cavities in the anterior teeth where aesthetics were important. Bio-material research has greatly improved the properties of the white filling materials (composites) and they are now available in a variety of shades, and are strong enough to be used in restoring small cavities in the posterior teeth where functional forces can be considerable.

Other white filling materials known as glass ionomer cements have been developed to be used in restoring small cavities in permanent posterior and deciduous teeth. Their main use has been in the restoration of abrasion (V-shaped) cavities in the necks of teeth where recession has occurred, and in areas where root decay has developed. Root decay is especially seen in the older age groups now that teeth are being retained longer. Glass ionomer cements release fluoride and therefore help to prevent secondary decay occurring at the junction between the restorative material and the cavity wall. (See Figures 19–21 on pages 60–61.)

Composites and glass ionomer cements require little or no cavity preparation prior to their insertion, but do require a dry field in order to gain adequate retention. It is normal practice with composite and glass ionomer filling materials for the enamel remaining around the edges of the cavity to be etched with an acid. This process provides a pitted surface into which the composite can flow, thus improving retention and marginal seal of the restoration. Glass ionomer cements also bond to dentine by way of their adhesive properties.

In large cavities, especially in premolar and molar teeth, pins may be utilised to help retain a core built up in amalgam, composite or glass ionomer

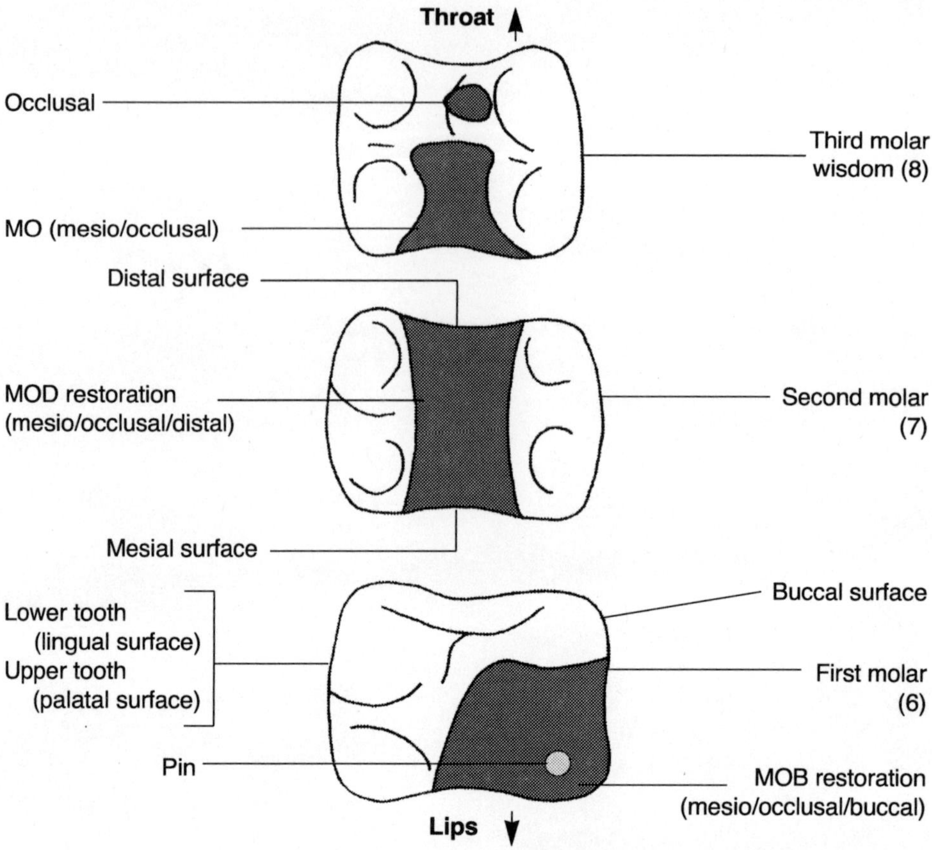

Figure 19. Bird's eye view of three molars with different surfaces restored.

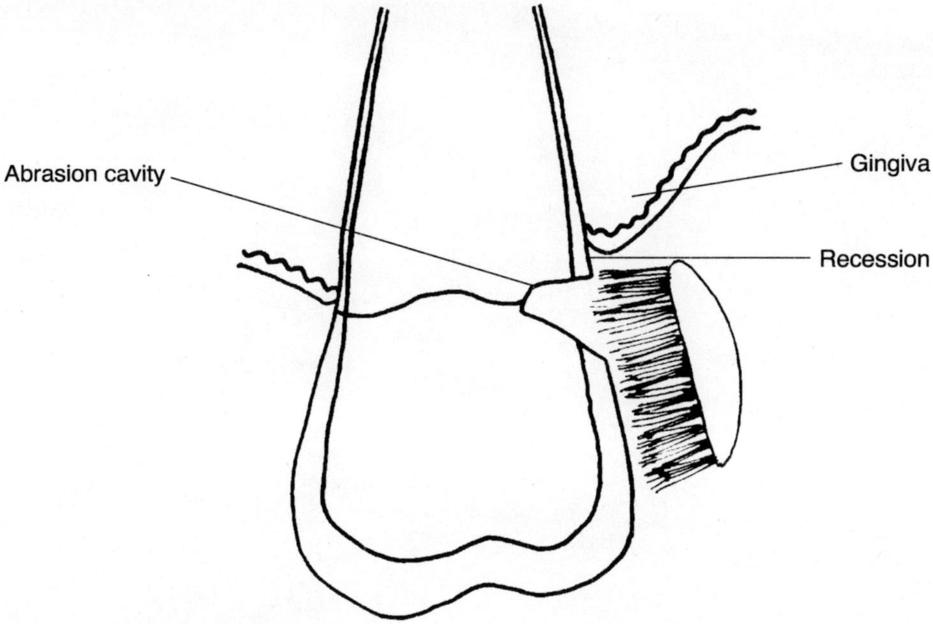

Figure 20. Above: section through a tooth with an abrasion cavity formed by over-zealous brushing. Below: the restored abrasion cavity.

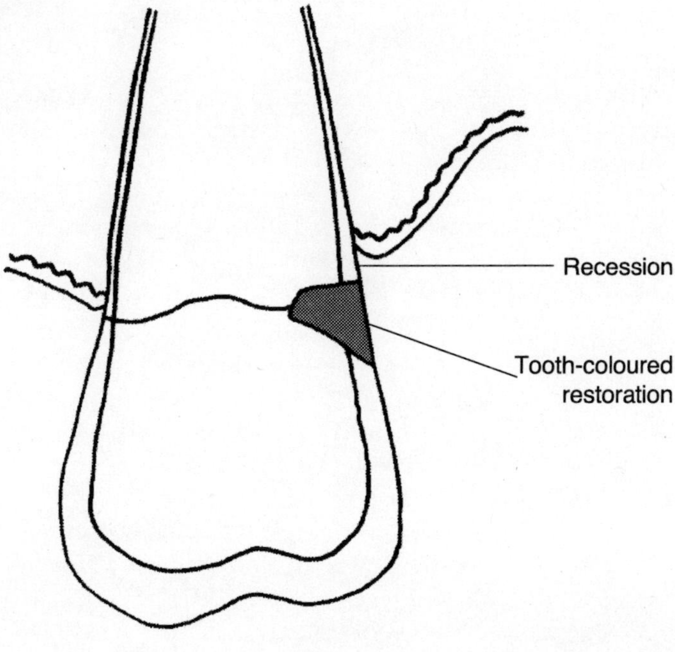

cement. This might be followed by preparing the tooth to accept some form of crown (cap).

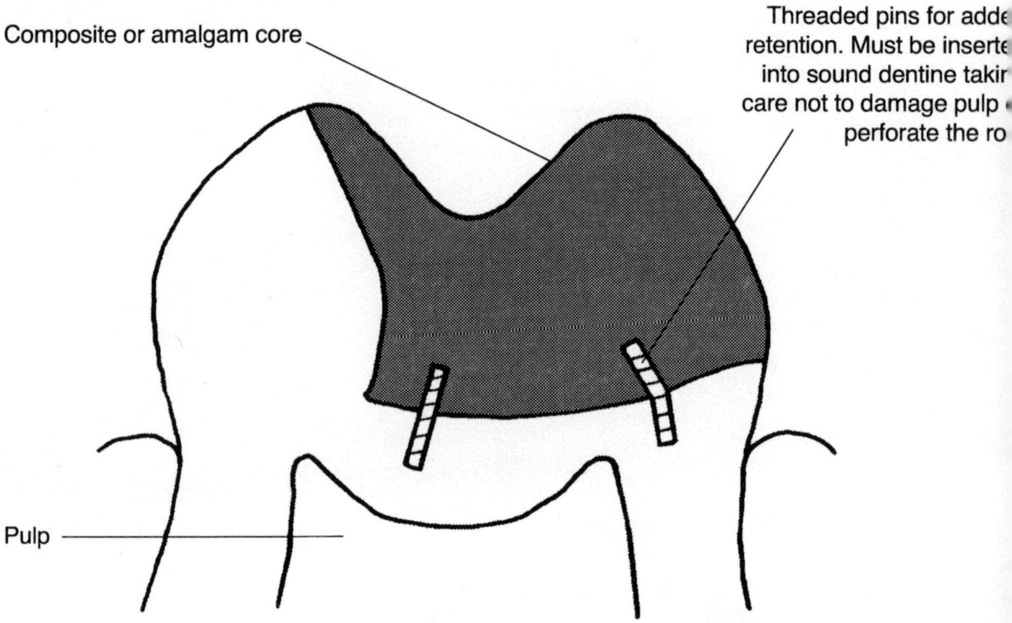

Figure 21. Section through a heavily restored molar prior to crowning.

With the advent of these white filling materials, the need for added retention from pins for restoring fractured anterior teeth became redundant as the remaining enamel could now be etched. When used together with various bonding agents (resins), a very retentive and aesthetic restoration can now be carried out. Most of the white filling materials are now hardened (cured) by light, using a 'light gun', or a combination of light and chemical reaction.

More recently there has been considerable improvement in the restoration of large cavities in posterior teeth with the advent of composite inlays which can either be fabricated in the surgery or in a laboratory. These are white (composite) fillings prepared on a stone model (die) made from an impression of the cavity. The composite is packed into the cavity and a special light box is used to cure the restoration under pressure before being bonded into the cavity with an adhesive.

Cavities can also be restored in porcelain utilising porcelain inlays (precast fillings), which are fabricated in the laboratory after an impression has been taken of the prepared tooth. The porcelain inlays show markedly good strength, are aesthetically pleasing and are bonded into prepared cavities utilising a composite resin material and a light-curing source.

With material used to restore teeth, expertise is required in order to provide a restoration which seals the cavity and does not leave a gap for bacterial plaque to gain access and give rise to secondary decay.

Problems arise in very deep cavities, especially if the decay extends below the gingivae and eventually onto the root face. These areas can be difficult to restore, especially if the matrix band, which is used as a form of 'shuttering', cannot be tightened around the tooth adequately to provide a seal when the material is packed into the cavity. If the band fails to adapt to the tooth at the bottom of the cavity there is the potential for material to be forced out into the surrounding tissues forming a ledge or overhang, or the bottom of the cavity may be left unfilled leaving a residual defect prone to further decay. The same problem may arise using white filling materials in anterior teeth. For the latter, the matrix band is usually hand held and is fabricated out of transparent celluloid, so that the material underneath can be cured with the light source. Difficulties may arise with moisture control, especially if the cavity is deep and extends below the gum, as this area may be inflamed, resulting in bleeding into the cavity and therefore reducing the chances of maintaining a dry field in order to retain the white filling material.

Cavities, large or small, can also be restored in gold, though on account of their expense and the introduction of more aesthetically coloured materials, the number of gold fillings or inlays has decreased. A well fitting gold inlay, however, is an exceptionally good restoration and can last for many years without the need for renewal.

CROWNS (CAPS)

Before the introduction of aluminous porcelain with its translucent properties and its increased strength, most teeth which required crowning, ie those which were heavily restored, were crowned in gold. Gold is extremely strong in thin section and has the added property of being able to be burnished and polished at the margins in order to gain good marginal adaptation with the tooth. Also, with the high content of gold the material was inert and did not corrode in the mouth. Full gold crowns are basically thimbles of metal which are constructed in the laboratory after an impression has been taken of the prepared tooth. A definite finishing line is left at the neck of the prepared tooth so that the technician can construct the gold thimble accurately on a stone model (die). Other types of gold crowns are sometimes constructed depending on the amount of tooth which has been destroyed. Hence, one may often find three quarter gold crowns which cover a large area of the prepared tooth, but leaving one outside wall intact. The need to remove a large amount of tooth structure is greatly reduced with the use of gold compared to other materials such as porcelain and porcelain bonded to metal.

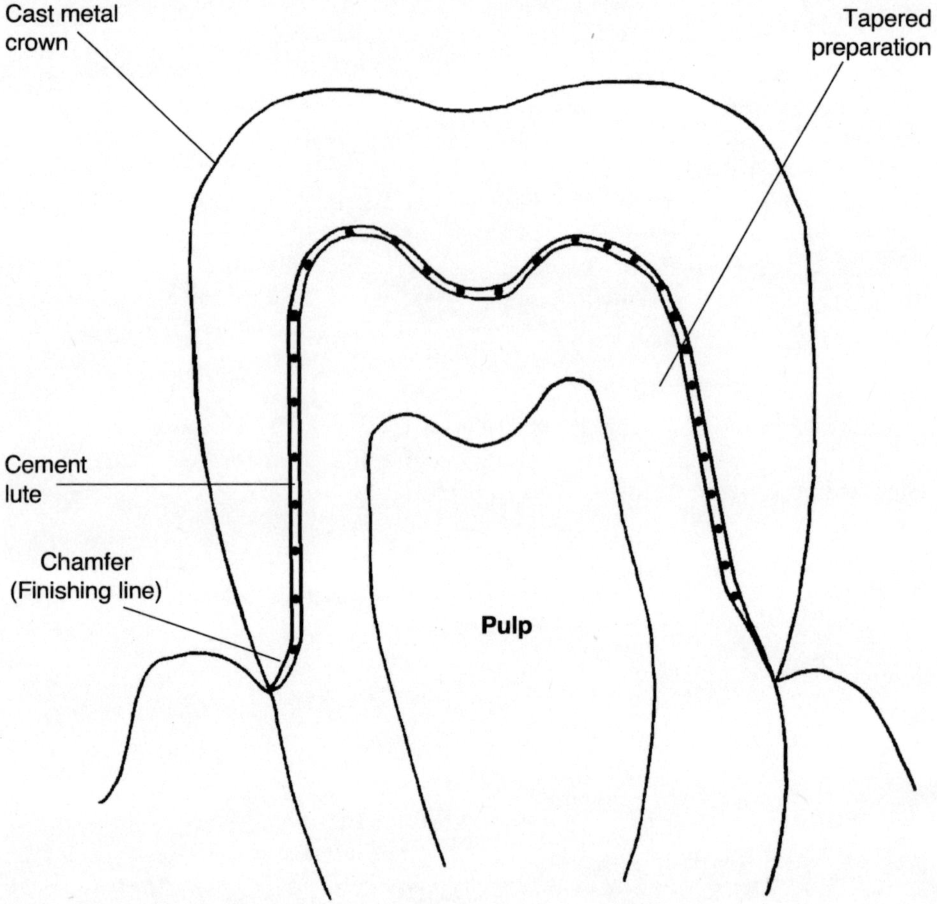

Figure 22. Section through a crowned tooth.

With the advent of improved porcelains, which are stronger, crowns can be fabricated for use in the front of the mouth where appearance or aesthetics are important. Various shades of porcelain are manufactured and a shade guide can be used in order to match the relevant teeth with a specific shade of porcelain. The problem with all porcelain crowns concerns the forces of the opposing teeth, especially if the lower front teeth are in close contact with the palatal or tongue surfaces of the upper front teeth, as this could lead to fractures. In areas where there is a likelihood of the opposing teeth fracturing the porcelain crowns, a metal framework is first constructed in a laboratory onto which the porcelain is laid down before being fired in an oven.

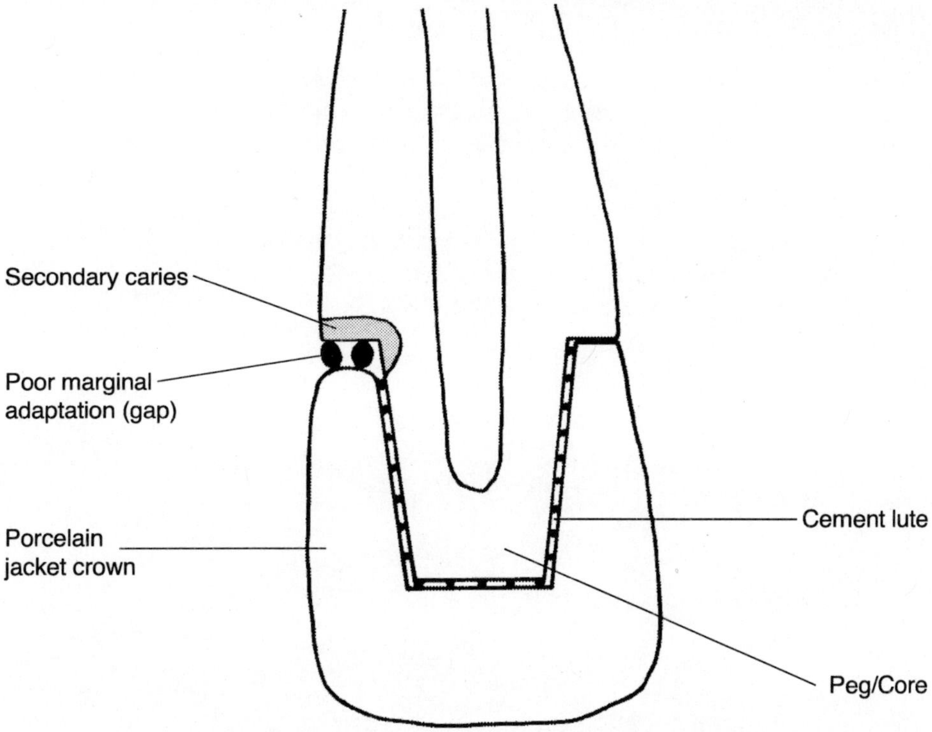

Figure 23. Section through a crowned anterior tooth.

Porcelain can be bonded onto either a non-precious or precious metal sub-structure which can then be fitted over prepared teeth in the anterior or posterior regions of the mouth. As in the case of gold crowns, the tooth is prepared, 'cut down to a peg' and an impression taken so that the porcelain-bonded-to-metal crown can be constructed by the laboratory and then fitted.

When preparing the relevant teeth for porcelain or porcelain-bonded-to-metal crowns, a greater amount of tooth structure needs to be removed in order to create enough space for an adequate thickness of porcelain as well as the metal sub-structure. The use of gold requires far less tooth reduction, although with gold being aesthetically unacceptable in the anterior part of the mouth, the use of porcelain-bonded-to-metal crowns is desirable.

If a tooth has been heavily restored or has decayed to such an extent that a normal restoration is not feasible, then one must consider other forms of crowns which utilise the root canal for added retention. The root canal is prepared (as detailed in the section on endodontics) for retaining some form of metal post so that a crown can be constructed and fitted onto it. Posts can be divided into two groups.

(a) Cast metal posts – the root canal is widened down to a specific length, which should be enough to provide adequate retention for a crown during function. A post of adequate length must be constructed, and this is usually carried out in the laboratory after an impression has been taken of the prepared root canal. A post is fabricated together with a metal core or peg so that this can be used as a foundation for a crown to be fitted over it. It is important to have posts of adequate length and thickness in order to prevent the posts becoming loose during function and to prevent fractures of the posts occurring in the root canals.

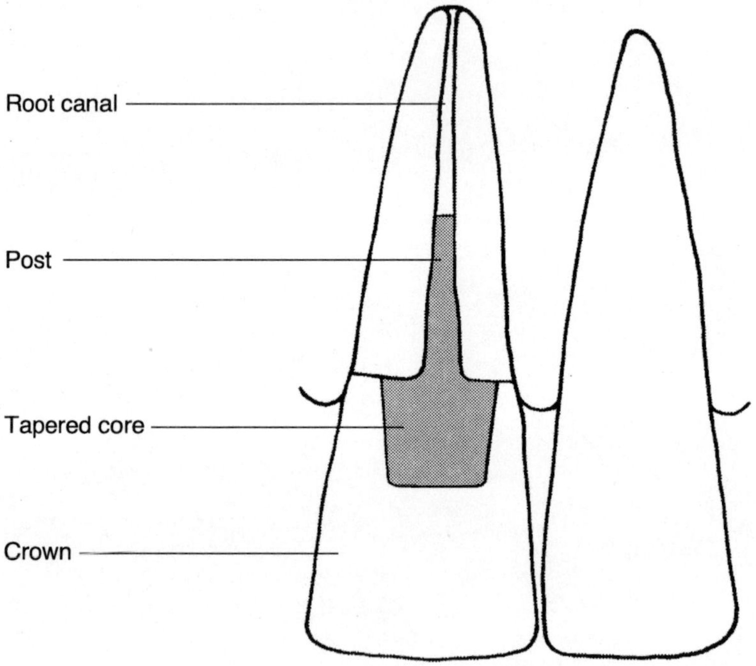

Figure 24. Cast post-retained crown.

(b) Preformed posts – are available in kits, together with the twist drill and taps to match the corresponding post and core. The posts are often screwed and cemented into place. The cores (pegs) are then built up in composite filling material followed by an impression for the crown to be made in the laboratory. All the crowns are usually cemented in place utilising a variety of cements such as zinc phosphate, glass ionomer and polycarboxylates.

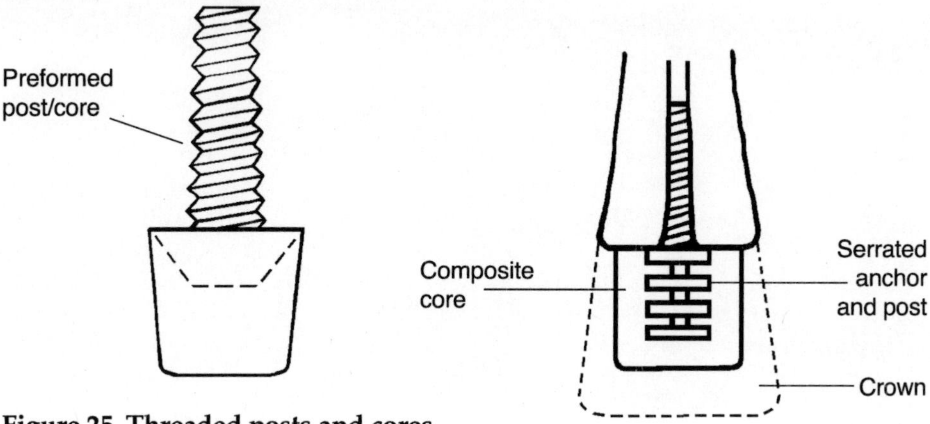

Figure 25. Threaded posts and cores.

Crowns may fail, come loose or fall off on account of poor tooth preparation, ie:

(a) from a lack of clinical height remaining after the tooth has been prepared, thus leaving very little area for retention; or

(b) by leaving the sides of the preparation too convergent, resulting in a conical shape lacking in retention, like a tee-pee tent.

Once a tooth has been prepared for a crown, the occlusal or biting surface will be reduced in height so that enough room is created to allow the technician to construct a crown of adequate thickness to restore the biting or occlusal surface of the tooth and interdigitate with the opposing tooth. Less space is required for gold restorations in contrast to porcelain-bonded-to-metal, which needs greater occlusal reduction in order to create enough room for the metal sub-structure and an adequate thickness of porcelain.

For recording the 'bite' or occlusal record, the majority of dental practitioners use a soft wax wafer which is placed on the biting surface of the prepared tooth and extended onto adjacent unprepared teeth, with the patient closing together into maximum interdigitation. In recent years other materials have been developed, such as quick-setting pastes and silicone rubbers which are much softer and provide a more accurate occlusal record.

If an inaccurate bite or occlusal record is taken, a crown will be constructed which will prevent the patient from interdigitating the teeth together. This will result in having to remove a considerable amount of porcelain or metal, resulting in a loss of contour and, in severe cases, perforation of the metal, exposing the underlying tooth.

Accurate impressions cannot be over-emphasised. The technician requires details of the preparation together with definite finishing lines (margins or shoulders) so that he/she can construct an accurately fitting crown that has no marginal discrepancies such as gaps which can lead to secondary decay occurring. There are many types of impression materials, though most dental practitioners use ones based on silicone rubber.

BRIDGEWORK

Where a tooth is missing, the teeth on either side of the gap can be used as abutments (pillars) for the provision of a bridge. In some cases, one tooth adjacent to the space can be utilised to form a cantilever bridge, eg lateral incisor cantilevered from a canine. Where considerable spaces exist, if enough teeth are still present around the dental arch then full arch complex bridgework can be constructed which may extend around from one side to the other, either as one unit or in sections. The sections may well be fixed together with screws (screw blocks) or by a variety of precision attachments mentioned in the prosthetics chapter. Bridgework and removable partial dentures can also be utilised together, but in many cases precision attachments are integrated into the bridgework providing the prosthesis with greater retention and stability. These large span cases of bridgework, with or without precision attachments and partial dentures, are very difficult to undertake and require a great deal of clinical skill and technical expertise, and should not be undertaken by inexperienced dental practitioners.

Bridgework can be divided into: fixed-fixed; fixed-movable; cantilever; spring cantilever; and adhesive – Maryland or Rochette.

Fixed-fixed

This is a rigid structure cemented to prepared teeth, adjacent to a space where a tooth has been lost. A three-unit bridge describes a false tooth (pontic) rigidly suspended by crowns at both ends of the space cemented onto prepared teeth (abutments). Note that more than one pontic may be used and more than one abutment tooth at either end may be employed.

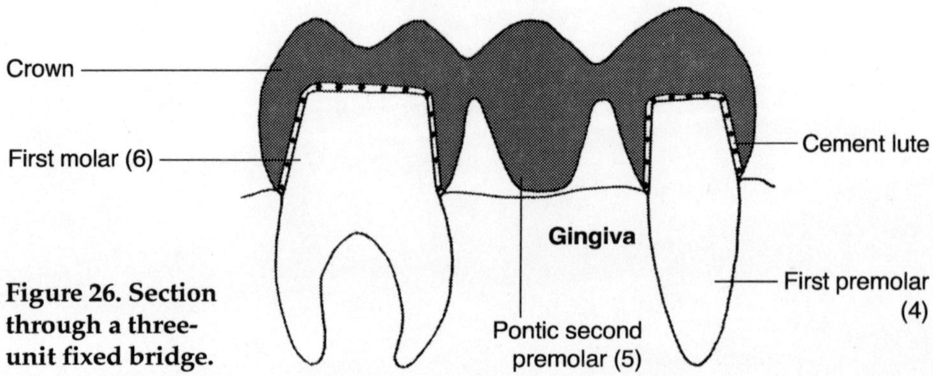

Figure 26. Section through a three-unit fixed bridge.

Fixed-movable

This is similar to the fixed-fixed structures but fabricated in two parts and joined together by way of a dovetail joint.

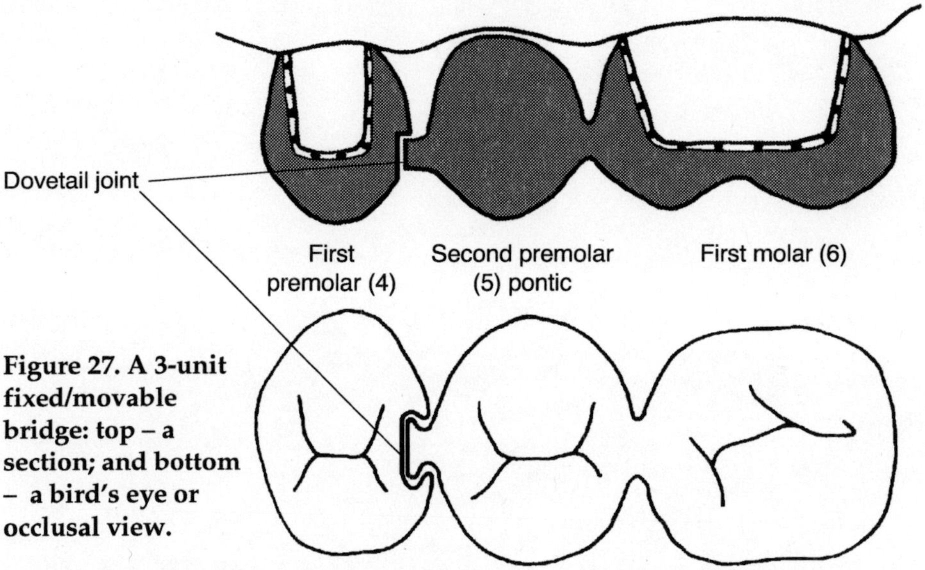

Figure 27. A 3-unit fixed/movable bridge: top – a section; and bottom – a bird's eye or occlusal view.

Cantilever

This is a rigid structure in which a single tooth adjacent to a space is prepared, crowned, and a pontic (two-unit bridge) suspended from it; eg a missing lateral incisor replaced by a pontic suspended or cantilevered from the adjacent canine tooth which has been prepared for a crown, normally a porcelain bonded to metal structure.

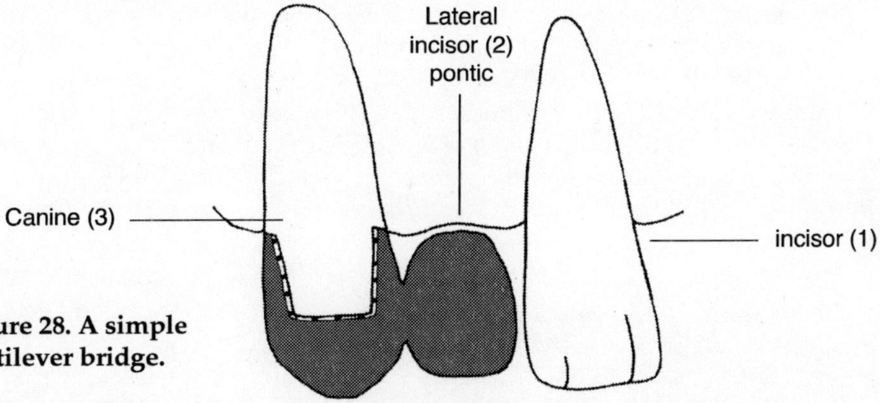

Figure 28. A simple cantilever bridge.

Spring cantilever

This is rarely seen today. It describes a pontic replacing a lost tooth and connected to a crown/crowns by a gold bar; it is useful for teeth which are spaced apart and therefore cannot be restored with a conventional bridge. If a missing tooth leaves a space greater than the tooth that was lost in an area of aesthetic importance, a porcelain pontic can be constructed behind which is a bar that runs across the palate where it is fused to a crown/crowns on one or more posterior teeth.

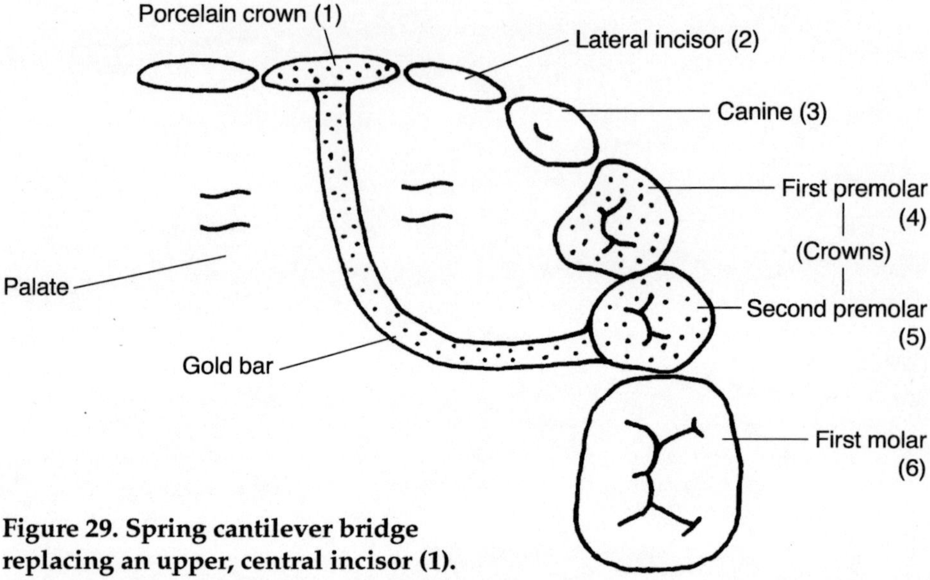

Figure 29. Spring cantilever bridge replacing an upper, central incisor (1).

Adhesive bridges

With the advent of adhesive materials such as composites and glass ionomer cements, their properties have been utilised for retaining simple bridges, providing the opposing teeth do not interfere or occlude closely with the abutment teeth being used. Maryland bridges consist of metal wings which are bonded to the lingual (tongue) side of the teeth, suspending a false tooth (pontic) either cantilevered or as a fixed-fixed structure (three units). They are particularly useful in the anterior part of the mouth where a single tooth may be missing and the adjacent teeth are decay or restoration free, thus preventing the need for excessive tooth removal which occurs when preparing a peg for the relevant crowns.

In the past, if a bridge was required in the front of the mouth then the adjacent teeth would need to be cut down to 'pegs' in order to accept porcelain-bonded-to-metal crowns, resulting in considerable loss of tooth structure. If the teeth were 'virginal' at the time of preparation the use of the Maryland type of bridge would prevent gross destruction of the teeth. Careful assessment of these cases needs to be carried out prior to undertaking the Maryland type of bridge as it depends on the wings being bonded to the relevant teeth by way of a composite. As with all composite filling materials, the enamel needs to be etched with acid in order to create a pitted surface which will increase the surface area for retaining the light-cured/chemically activated composite cement. Improvement of the composite and glass ionomer materials has greatly increased retention and, in certain situations, posterior teeth such as premolars can also be replaced using a Maryland type of bridge. Hopefully in the future the need for gross reduction of posterior teeth for crowns will become greatly reduced.

Minor preparation is carried out to the teeth to be used for retaining the wings, followed by an accurate impression which is sent to the laboratory for fabrication of the bridge. The laboratory sandblasts or etches the metal surface of the wings with an acid, to give a pitted surface and provide a greater surface area with which the cement can bond. Together with the etched tooth surface a substantial bond can be acquired, and a bridge of this type can be retained for a number of years. As these bridges are technique sensitive, there are a number of occasions when, unfortunately, they do become separated from the teeth and therefore require re-etching in the laboratory before being re-bonded to the relevant teeth.

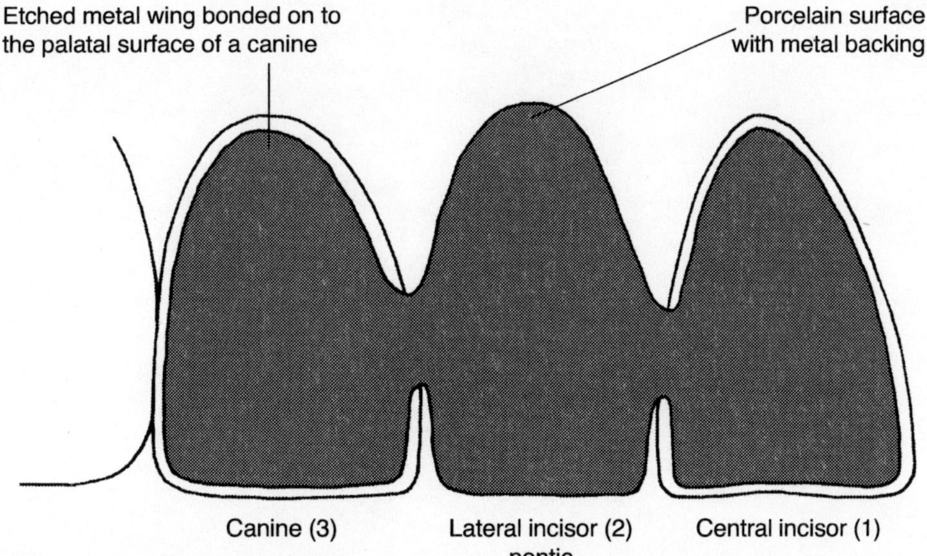

Figure 30. A Maryland bridge.

The Rochette bridge

This is similar in design to the Maryland bridge but the wings are perforated, allowing the bonding material (composites) to be forced through the perforations to form tags. These mechanically retain the bridge on the teeth. The teeth themselves are etched with an acid but the metalwork is not, thus leaving the perforations for mechanical retention. The Rochette bridge has been largely superseded by the Maryland bridge, but it still has a useful place in restorative dentistry as a temporary/semi-permanent bridge in areas where a conventional bridge would be unsuitable. For example, teeth immediately adjacent to the space to be replaced with a false tooth/pontic may be showing signs of increased mobility due to the ravages of periodontal disease, resulting in considerable loss of supporting bone around the roots. These teeth would not be suitable for preparing crowns for conventional bridgework but could be used for the Rochette type of bridge as they may have a limited prognosis. Adhesive bridges provide a simpler and a very much cheaper alternative.

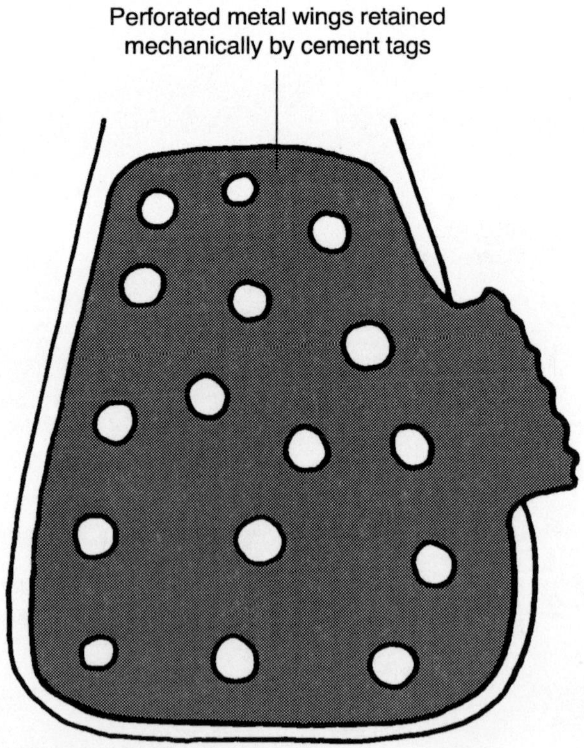

Figure 31. A Rochette bridge.

Temporary bridges

When teeth are prepared for crowns or bridgework, temporary crowns should be fitted in order to prevent over-eruption and unwanted movement. Failure to prevent this occurring will more often than not lead to a bridge framework which will not seat accurately on the prepared teeth, resulting in major adjustments being required or a new impression being taken. Temporary bridges are usually constructed in acrylic (plastic) and cemented in place with a temporary cement, so that they can be easily removed when fitting the permanent crowns or bridgework.

With large span bridges involving many teeth, the bite or 'occlusion' can be extremely difficult to record. Accurate records of the occlusion are first taken and this information, together with a stone model taken from the impression of the prepared teeth and a plaster model of the opposing teeth, is transferred to a type of artificial jaws (articulator). Simple articulators will only allow simple hinge movement of the jaws, while more complex models will allow, to varying degrees, movement of the jaws both forwards and laterally, thereby approximately copying the movement of the jaws in the patient. In complex crown and bridgework cases this information is of importance to the technician in order for him to construct a bridge which allows movement of the jaws in all directions without any interferences occurring. Articulators also allow a new bite (occlusion) to be created which is stable and reproducible, in contrast to the occlusion prior to treatment which may have been difficult to locate and record, due to the loss of a number of posterior teeth which provide an accurate 'locating mechanism' when the teeth close together and interdigitate (see recording bite/occlusion in the chapter on prosthetics).

VENEERS

In recent years the introduction of porcelain veneers has, in many patients, reduced the necessity for removing large amounts of tooth structure for the provision of crowns. These restorations require minimal removal of tooth structure to provide a surface for the veneers to be bonded onto the labial surface of the tooth. The tooth preparation only involves removing a small amount of the enamel surface and, after an impression has been taken, the technician constructs a veneer to fit accurately on the face of the tooth. The veneers are similar to false fingernails and are bonded to the surface of the teeth with a composite filling material, once again after the tooth has been etched with acid. The bonding agent is then usually light-cured. These restorations are very useful for discoloured teeth or for the single in-standing front tooth which, by bonding with a veneer, would be brought back into alignment with the other adjacent anterior teeth, thus improving the overall appearance. Care must be taken of possible functional interferences from the opposing lower teeth, so there may be certain situations when these restorations should not be utilised. They are most commonly carried out on the six upper front teeth, although other situations, such as with upper premolars, may also be treated in this way.

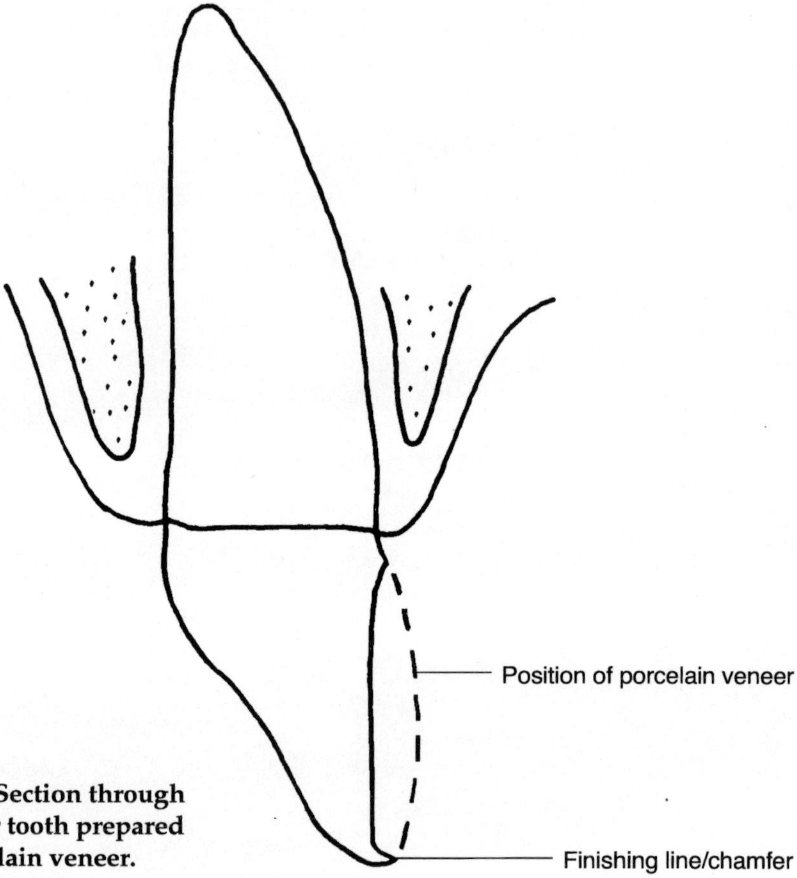

Figure 32. Section through an anterior tooth prepared for a porcelain veneer.

ENDODONTICS (ROOT CANAL TREATMENT)

The commonest cause of injury to the pulp chamber containing the nerves and blood vessels is dental caries. In a deep carious cavity bacteria are present, and it is considered that bacterial toxins (poisons) pass into the pulp causing inflammation to occur (pulpitis) and in most cases pain. Damage to the pulp can also be caused by a number of other factors:

(a) when preparing a cavity using a high-speed drill without coolant;

(b) by direct trauma – if this is severe the apical nerves and blood vessels are severed leading to death of the pulp contents and eventual necrosis. The crown of the tooth may or may not be fractured from the traumatic incident, and often with these injuries the tooth will die and necrosis may occur with no symptoms. The patient may notice the tooth becoming discoloured and only on routine X-ray will evidence of any infection become evident. It is important to note that this area of infection may well remain symptomless for many years, progressing slowly, and in a small number of cases may well resorb the surrounding bone and become very large.

Vitality tests

A number of tests are used in order to determine whether a tooth is alive or dead. If the tooth is non-vital there will be no response to certain stimuli, such a heat, cold, drilling or electricity. Conversely, if the tooth is vital then these various stimuli will give a painful response of varying degrees depending on the state of the tooth. Many of these teeth may have some pulp damage and hence the response to the stimuli may give abnormal readings that cannot be relied upon to confirm accurately whether a tooth is vital or not. These tests, however, are useful in trying to pinpoint a source of pain in a particular area of the mouth, although in many cases the tooth causing the symptoms can be diagnosed by a number of other factors as well, eg tender to percussion (TTP).

Root canal preparation and filling

The object of root canal treatment is to remove all the necrotic (dead) tissue within the pulp chamber and the root canal and create a seal from the surrounding tissues and oral cavity. Sealing the apex of the tooth prevents bacterial infestation occurring within the canal where it would be protected from the body's defence mechanism. If allowed to gain a hold, toxins are produced that filter out into the surrounding tissues and give rise to inflammation and subsequent abscess formation. It is important that the pulp chamber and root canal are cleaned mechanically in order to remove all the potential sources of infection. A variety of instruments (files and reamers) are used in order to clean and widen the root canal prior to inserting a definitive root filling.

Access is usually gained to the pulp chamber via a cavity cut through the biting surface of a molar or premolar tooth. In anterior teeth the access cavity is prepared through the lingual or palatal aspect of the tooth. Files in ascending diameters (numbered 8 to 120) are then used to clean and widen the canal system, together with copious use of irrigation (Milton or saline). Following instrumentation a clean, smooth and dry canal should be obtained before proceeding to the definitive root filling.

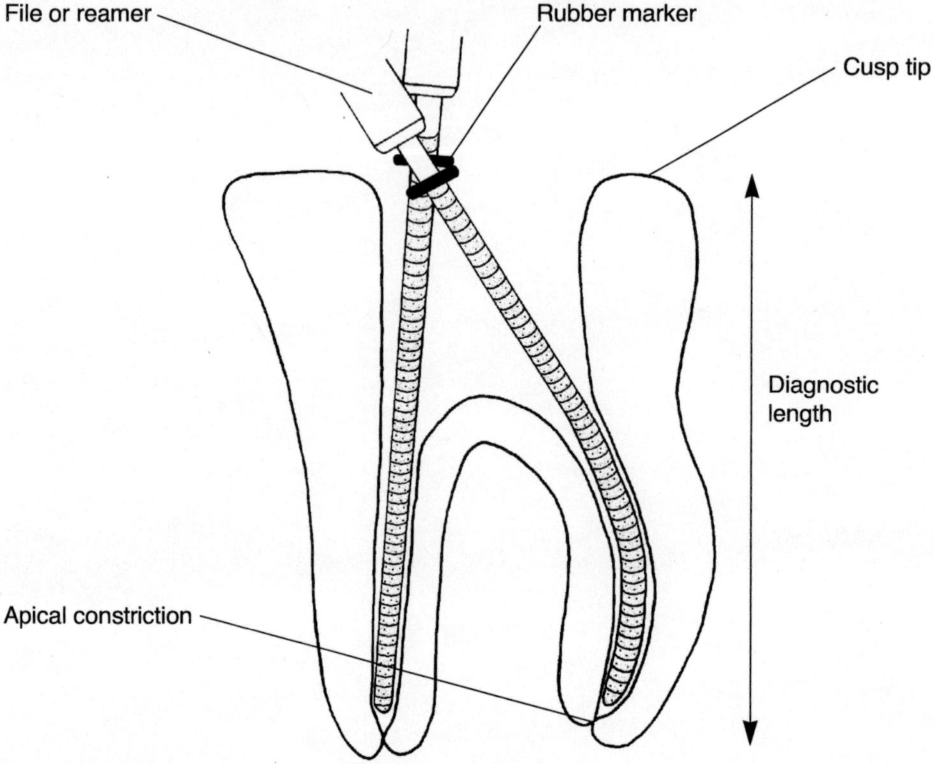

Figure 33. Cleaning and widening the root canal.

Root canal treatment should be carried out under the protection of a rubber dam. This is a square sheet of rubber which is fitted over the tooth after a small hole has been punched through it. The rubber dam is fixed in place with a clamp and the corners of the sheet fixed to a frame outside the patient's mouth. All students are taught how to use a rubber dam since not only does it protect the tooth from potential contamination of saliva, it also safeguards the patient against the loss of small instruments which may be easily swallowed or inhaled, particularly if the treatment is carried out in the posterior part of the mouth and the patient is in the supine position.

In instances where an instrument is swallowed it is usually sufficient to monitor progress through the digestive tract until it is finally expelled; this rarely causes problems. If the small instruments are inhaled, however, they need to be retrieved; although this can often be done via bronchoscopy, there is always the possibility of a surgical procedure being required.

After the access cavity has been made into the pulp chamber, a fine file is inserted down the root canal towards the apex and an X-ray is taken. The X-ray, together with a file in place, is used to provide adequate information regarding the length of the canal so that subsequent instrumentation may take place as far as, but not through, the apex of the root (Diagnostic X-ray). Tables are available for the average lengths of teeth as a guide prior to taking the initial X-ray. Once a clean, dry and widened root canal has been obtained and the correct length established (working length), the canal may be sealed up using gutta-percha, which is cemented into place with a non-irritant cement. Gutta-percha is manufactured as measured, thin sections called points, and the sizes match those of the files for easier assessment of the size required to fill the canal. A number of dental practitioners still use silver points, especially in fine canals, though their use is not now taught in dental schools. (See Plate 2, page 53. 5| or 15 root filled.)

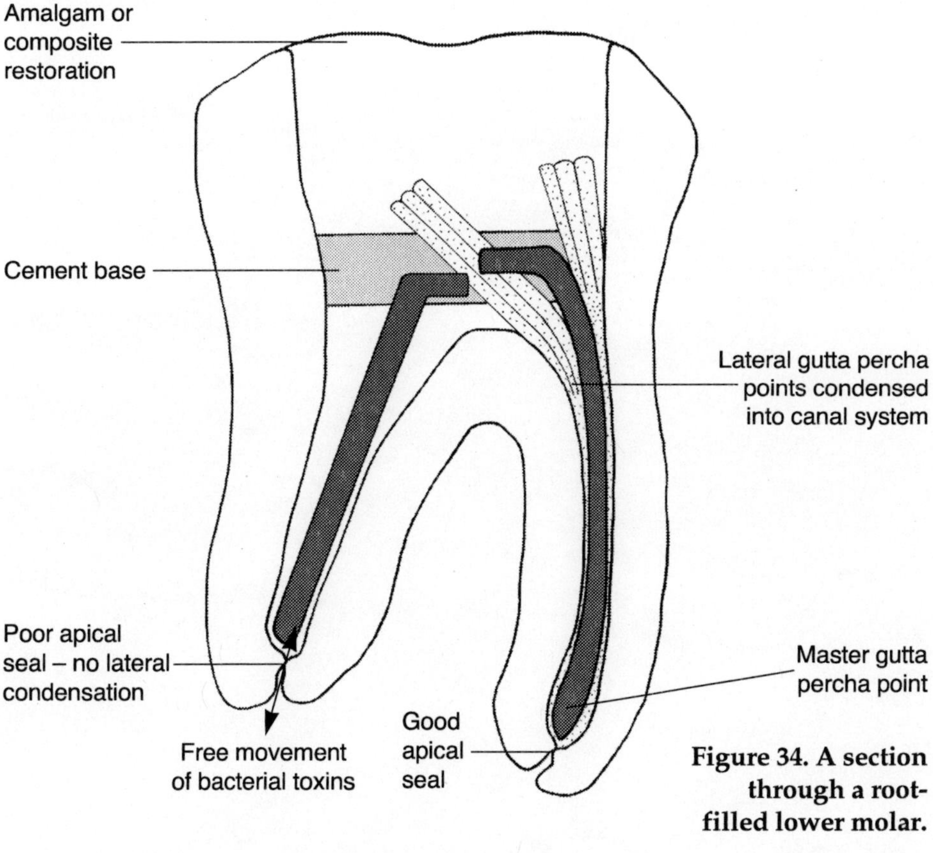

Figure 34. A section through a root-filled lower molar.

If a tooth has been severely infected, with a certain amount of pus present during instrumentation, then after cleaning and irrigation has been carried out an antiseptic dressing may be inserted for up to a few days in order to help remove the remaining bacteria before proceeding to cleaning and preparing the canal in the usual way. After the root filling has been cemented in place and an adequate apical seal obtained, the tooth can be restored. If an apical seal has not been achieved the root treatment will probably fail, resulting in re-infection and symptoms. In these cases remedial root canal treatment will become necessary. Even under ideal circumstances root canal fillings are not 100% successful, and therefore on occasion teeth will require extracting. In some circumstances a surgical procedure is carried out to sustain a seal at the end of the root. This procedure is called an apicectomy, and is discussed further under the section on oral surgery. Occasionally the contents of the pulp chamber may need to be removed electively so that the root canal can be utilised for incorporating various types of metal post.

CHAPTER ELEVEN

TREATMENT OF PERIODONTAL DISEASE

SUMMARY

- Build up of bacterial plaque at the necks of the teeth quickly leads to inflammation and the establishment of gingivitis.
- The inflammation and bleeding resulting from gingivitis can be completely eliminated by the removal of the plaque.
- Plaque consists of a complex mass of bacteria within a matrix of complex sugars.
- Chronic gingivitis eventually leads to chronic periodontitis and the destruction of the supporting tissues, ie the periodontal ligament and the alveolar bone. Progress is usually painless over many years and may only become noticeable when the patient becomes aware of increased looseness of the teeth, drifting, or the advent of an acute periodontal abscess.
- Tissue damage resulting from bacterial plaque is caused by a variety of enzymes and toxins (poisons) produced by the bacteria.
- Malfunction of the immunological system may also be an important factor in the progress of periodontal disease. Patients with depressed immune systems, such as in AIDS, may be characterised by greatly enhanced destruction of the periodontal tissues.
- Certain systemic disorders may also exacerbate the disease process, eg diabetes and Down's syndrome.

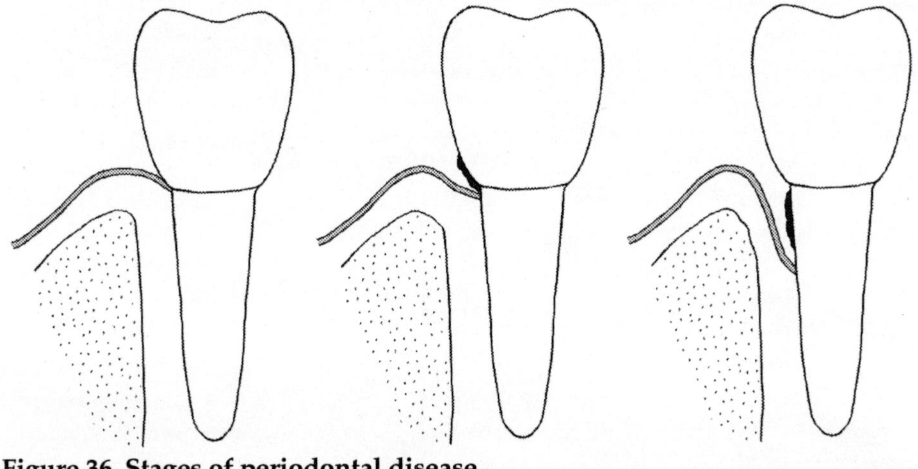

Figure 36. Stages of periodontal disease.

CHRONIC GINGIVITIS

The basis of all treatment is the control of dental plaque. If oral hygiene is of a high standard then this will result in a healthy mouth with the gingivae reverting to a pink, stippled morphology (form) closely bound down to the necks of the teeth. Correct use of a toothbrush and the various dental aids such as floss, woodsticks and inter-proximal brushes all have an important function in maintaining the cervical and inter-proximal areas free of plaque.

Localised areas of inflammation which do not respond to routine oral hygiene methods may require further investigations in order to ascertain whether other local factors may be exacerbating the problem. Carious cavities, poor contacts between adjacent teeth (food packing sites) and poorly contoured restorations (ledges) may all encourage the accumulation of bacterial plaque. Other forms of treatment, eg the renewal of restorations, may therefore be required in order to provide sites which can be easily cleaned.

If areas of calculus are present, which also increases plaque retention, routine scaling should be carried out at the same time as oral hygiene instruction is given. Scaling may take the form of hand instrumentation utilising various designs of hand scalers designed to remove deposits adequately from all areas of the mouth. Most practices also use ultrasonic/air scalers which, under a water coolant, vibrate the deposits from the teeth. Many dentists and hygienists use both methods of scaling during treatment.

ACUTE ULCERATIVE GINGIVITIS

Most cases of acute ulcerative gingivitis are seen in patients who already have an underlying chronic gingivitis due to a lack of adequate oral hygiene. This condition is rarely seen in patients who possess a high standard of oral hygiene and healthy periodontal tissues.

It is important therefore that oral hygiene is improved to a high standard and all deposits of calculus/tartar are removed from the necks of the teeth. In severe cases where the patients may be run down and under stress, they may become pyrexic and possess an associated swelling of the nearby lymph glands (submandibular lymphadenopathy). Besides improving oral hygiene and removing the gross deposits, antibiotics may be required, for which Metronidazole is the antibiotic of choice in these cases. Antiseptic mouthwashes may also be used, eg hydrogen peroxide, sodium perborate (Bocasan), Corsodyl, Difflam and Listerine, etc.

This condition soon clears up with conservative measures but the knife-edged papillae at the infection site will be lost. Therefore gingival morphology will more often than not appear aesthetically displeasing due to recession and the flattening of the gingival papillae.

ACUTE GINGIVITIS (LOCAL TRAUMA, BURNS)

These conditions usually heal without any complications after the irritant has been removed. Occasionally the use of antiseptic mouthwashes may be prescribed in order to prevent secondary infection occurring.

CHRONIC PERIODONTITIS

If chronic gingivitis is allowed to progress the specialised epithelial attachment at the base of the gingival sulcus (in health 0.5mm in depth when probed) will eventually break down. This will allow pocket formation to occur which will increase in depth slowly and painlessly over a number of years, more often than not without the patient being aware of any problem.

At the base of the pockets there is a conflict between the toxins produced by the bacterial plaque and the immune system of the host, and it is in this battlefield where further destruction of the tissues occurs, including resorption of the alveolar bone supporting the teeth.

As routine scaling and good oral hygiene will not eliminate the deposits on the root faces, more invasive treatment is required in order to eliminate the aetiological factors sustaining the disease process.

Root planing

This is normally carried out under local anaesthesia utilising ultrasonic scalers and/or specially designed instruments which are able to clean the root faces in all areas of the mouth, eg Gracey and Goldman-Fox curettes. These instruments engage the deposits on the root face and, by way of a vertical action, the cutting edge removes the calcified deposits. At the same time the pockets can be irrigated with various antiseptics, eg Corsodyl. After this treatment has been completed shrinkage of the gingival tissues will normally occur, together with a reduction in inflammation. A certain amount of recession will occur resulting in some exposure of the roots; at the same time pocket reduction will have taken place and hopefully the tissues will return to some form of healthy state. It is important to point out that bone will not return to its normal height and the connective tissue (fibrous) attachment freed from the roots during pocket formation will not normally re-attach to any extent, so by this stage no complete reversal of the disease process will occur. Patients will have sustained irreversible damage to the supporting tissues but hopefully, with regular maintenance, this fragile periodontal state can be sustained. The tissues around the cervical areas of the teeth after periodontal treatment has been carried out are very much more susceptible to further bacterial attack compared to the periodontal tissues with a normal

Figure 37. The removal of contaminated subgingival calculus and plaque from the root face of a deep pocket by (below) ultrasonic scaling and (right) hand instrumentation.

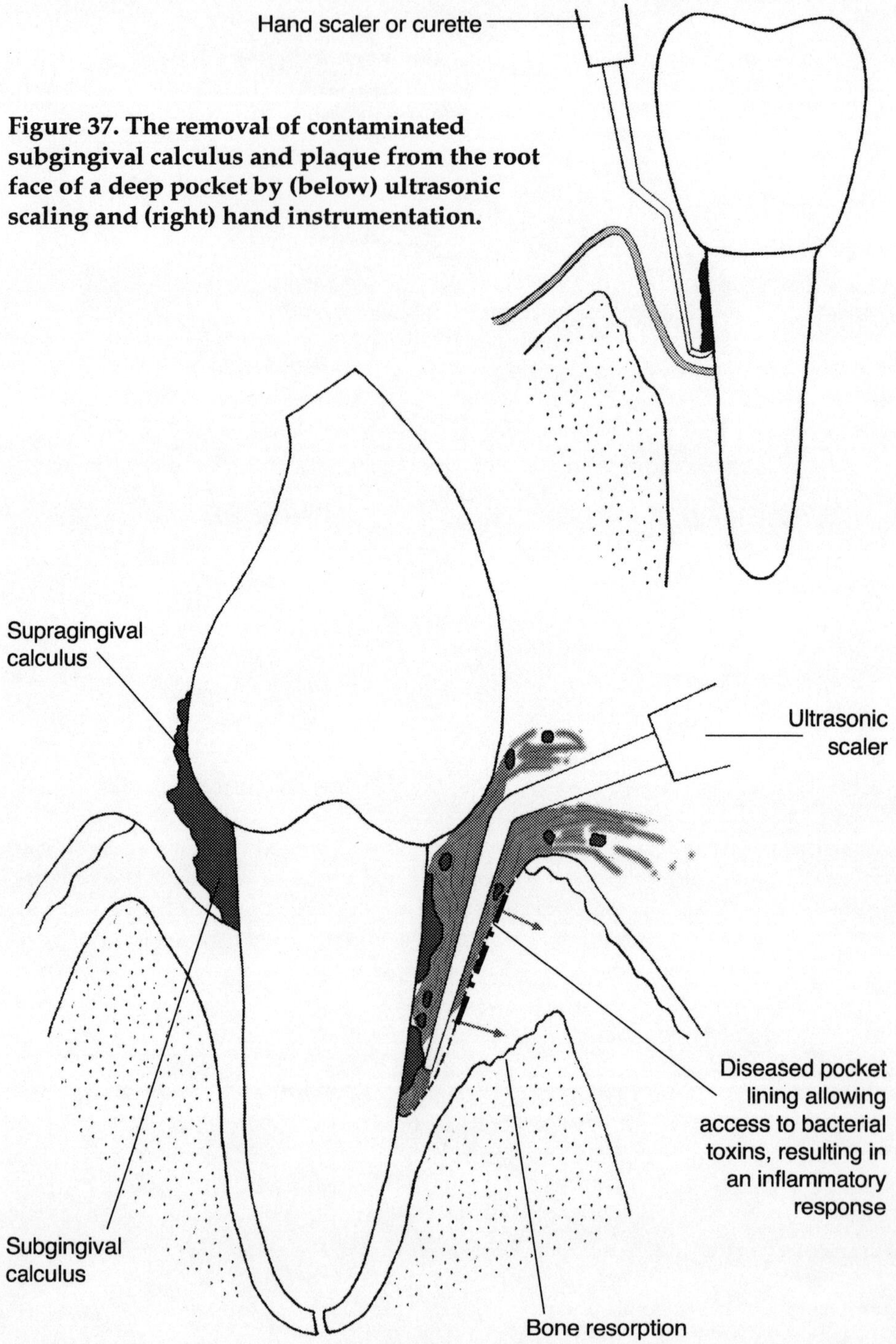

depth of gingival sulcus and an intact epithelial attachment. Therefore, if oral hygiene fails to be of an adequate standard there is a greater propensity for the tissues to break down further, leading to rapid pocket formation, bone loss and eventual increased mobility which will result in extractions becoming necessary.

As mentioned before, the disease process is normally painless and occurs over a long period of time, often not becoming noticeable until the patient complains of increased looseness of the teeth or the presence of an acute abscess originating from a deep and inaccessible pocket.

Unfortunately there are a few patients who do not respond well to treatment, even though plaque control is of a high standard and the root surfaces have been adequately cleaned. These cases are stubborn to normal methods of treatment and are now often referred to as 'refractory' periodontitis. Up to 10% of patients with periodontitis may come under this umbrella, and research into the aetiology of 'refractory' periodontitis has in recent years focussed on microbiology and the possibility of malfunction of the immune system. These are very unfortunate cases as teeth are often lost at an early age. All forms of treatment such as root planing and periodontal surgery, together with the use of systemic antibiotics, do not appear to slow down the disease process, and therefore a decision at some time has to be made as to whether periodontal therapy should be curtailed and extractions carried out followed by the provision of some form of prosthesis.

Surgery

Until a few years ago the treatment of pocketing involved the use of surgery which, in effect, removed the diseased part of the pocket lining and at the same time provided good visual access to the root faces so that a more thorough cleaning could be carried out. The raised envelope, or flap, of gingival tissue after treatment had been completed would be sutured back at a much lower level, so that the pockets would be completely eliminated but once complete healing had taken place significant areas of recession would be present.

Many studies have been carried out with a view to ascertaining whether root planing or surgery, or a combination of both, provide a more successful treatment outcome. It would appear that, whatever treatment methods are carried out, provided a high standard of plaque control is undertaken together with a regular maintenance programme provided by the dentist and/or hygienist, a successful result will be normally be acquired and the disease controlled.

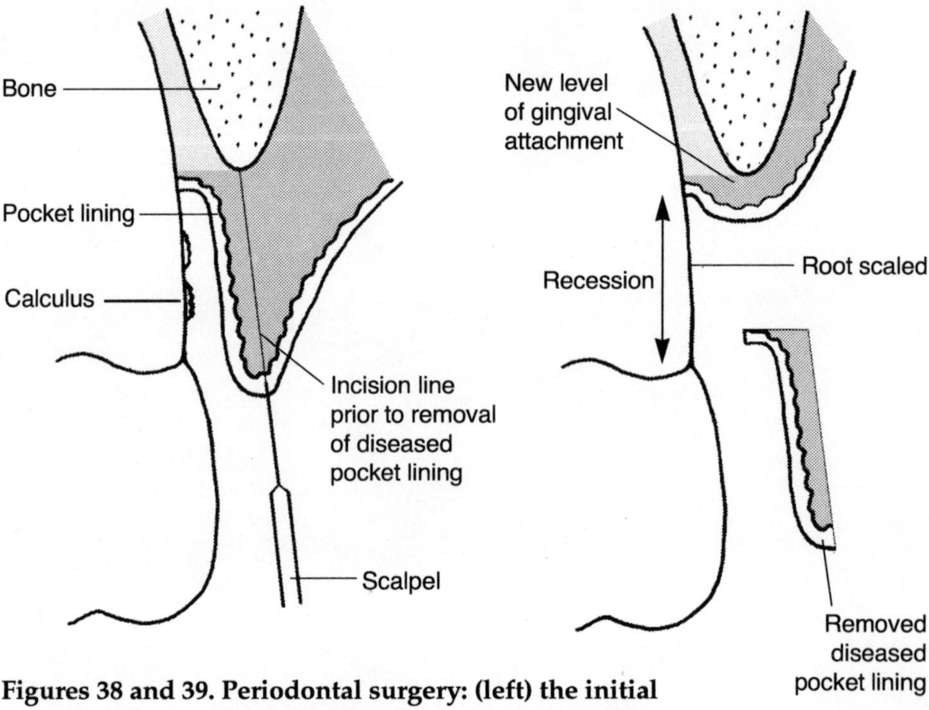

Figures 38 and 39. Periodontal surgery: (left) the initial incision prior to surgery; and (right) post-pocket elimination.

JUVENILE PERIODONTITIS

A considerable amount of research has been undertaken to find a cause for this condition. Research has focussed on the bacterial flora as well as possible defects in the host's immunological system.

Epidemiological studies appear to suggest that juvenile periodontitis is much more common in people of Afro-Caribbean descent. There is also a possibility that susceptibility is genetically determined.

Treatment for this condition is the same as for chronic periodontitis, though extractions may be necessary where teeth cannot be saved.

CHAPTER TWELVE

PROSTHETICS

Prosthetics involves the replacing of missing teeth by artificial ones. These may be full dentures (false teeth) where the patient is totally edentulous, or partial dentures where only one or more teeth are missing. Replacing missing teeth with dentures restores the normal appearance and improves mastication and speech. Most dentures, whether full or partial, are constructed out of acrylic (plastic) together with acrylic teeth. Metal may be used for the framework of partial dentures and is usually an alloy of cobalt/chrome. This has replaced the use of gold for the framework on account of its lower costs.

FULL DENTURES

Dentures are constructed in a laboratory after impressions of the mouth have been taken and a number of stages are passed before the final fitting. These include measuring the relationship of the upper and lower jaws vertically and horizontally and recording this with an occlusal (bite) registration. This is necessary so that, when the final dentures are fitted, the patient does not end up 'over-closed' (finding his chin advancing towards the tip of his nose), or not closed enough. Both may give rise to pain in the temporomandibular joint due to muscle spasm created by the altered vertical dimension. For these reasons, accurate jaw relations are taken using a measuring gauge or pair of dividers, and after the occlusal or bite record has been taken the models are returned to the laboratory and mounted on an articulator which artificially mimics the movement of the jaws. These are essentially a hinged mechanism, although there are a number of more complex types on the market which have varying range of movements imitating more accurately the movements of the jaw. In most cases of denture construction, a simple hinge articulator is used to set up the artificial teeth in the correct vertical and horizontal dimension. The articulator shows in three dimensions the relationship of the lower jaw to the upper jaw and to the temporomandibular joint. The teeth are set up accordingly and the dentures are tried in the mouth with the teeth in wax only, and any adjustments made before the final processing in acrylic. Further appointments are given to adjust the dentures as often they may be traumatic to the soft tissues in the mouth and give rise to ulceration. These areas of increased pressure then need to be relieved.

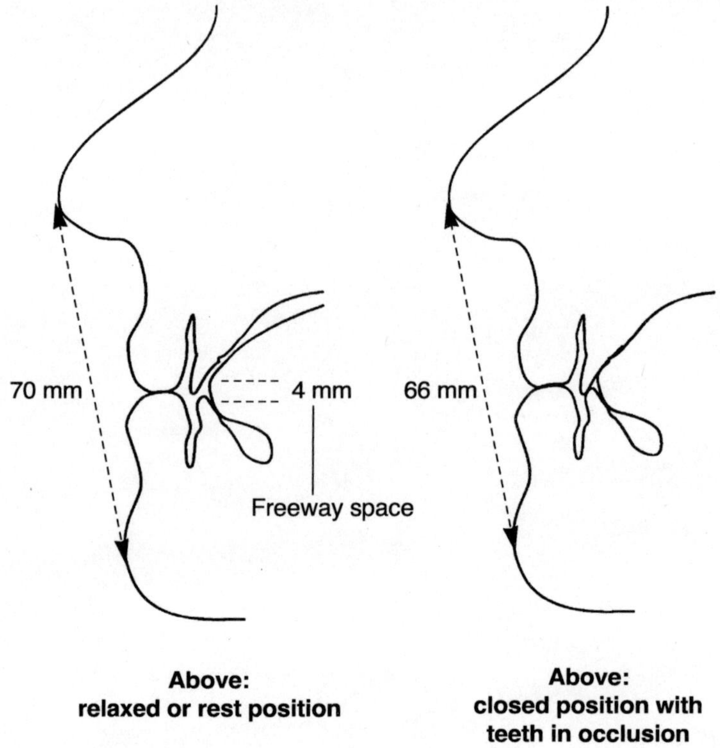

Figure 40. Correct vertical dimensions incorporated into a set of dentures.

PARTIAL DENTURES

As has been mentioned above, partial dentures may be completely constructed from acrylic or from a chrome/cobalt skeleton framework on which the artificial teeth are embedded into acrylic held in place on this metal framework. The technique for taking jaw relationships and occlusal or bite records is basically the same as with full dentures, using a temporary base plate and wax rim fitted into the mouth so that an accurate bite registration may be taken. If there are only a few teeth missing and the other teeth interdigitate adequately, then there may be no need to use these temporary base plates and blocks, but simply insert a wax wafer between the biting surface of the teeth so that, when the patient closes together, an accurate record of their relationship may be made. With a large number of teeth remaining in good contact the vertical dimensions of the face remain the same and there is no problem recording the facial height.

Many acrylic partial dentures fitted in the mouth are tissue borne, ie they rest upon the soft tissues in the mouth and do not use adjacent teeth for support. The chrome cobalt dentures, besides providing a framework around the teeth utilise the remaining teeth to provide retention and support for the prosthesis during mastication (clasps and rest seats). Clasps, in the form of wrought steel, can be incorporated into acrylic partial dentures to aid retention though there are many patients who prefer the dentures to be claspless. When teeth are removed the supporting bone gradually resorbs, thereby altering the shape of the jaw. This means that dentures that are fitted early after extractions may cease to fit adequately after a few months and need to be relined. This involves using the denture base as an impression tray, taking a further impression which, in effect, fills the gap between the original and new position of the bone and the space can then be filled in with new acrylic in the laboratory.

OVERDENTURES

Occasionally, patients may be left with two or more teeth which are sound and the roots well supported in bone. These can be utilised to provide increased retention for a denture by undertaking elective root canal treatment (see the chapter on endodontics) followed by resection of the remaining crowns of the teeth down to gum level. A variety of devices can then be incorporated into the remaining root to provide support and added retention to the overlying full denture.

The teeth most commonly used for overdentures are the canines, especially the lower canines, as it is the full lower denture which is the most difficult to retain and control. If certain teeth can be retained and utilised for further support and stability then this will certainly help the patient. Another

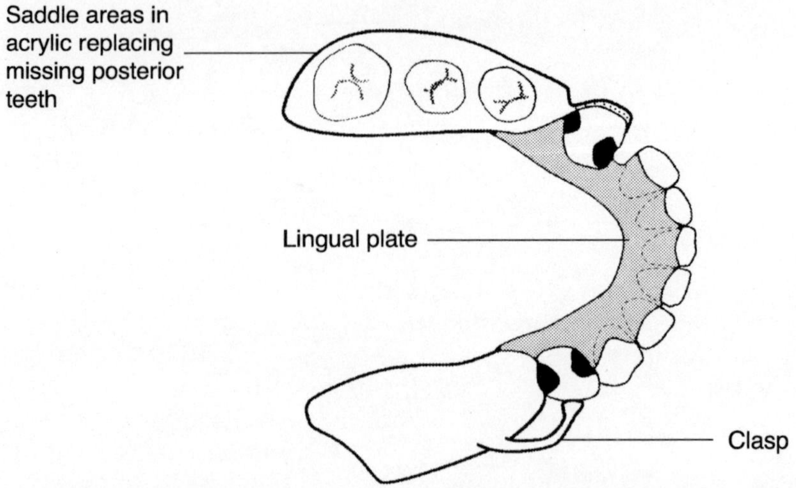

Figure 41. Designs for chrome-cobalt metal partial dentures: (above) lower prosthesis replacing 7 6 5 | 5 6 7; (below) upper prosthesis replacing four front teeth 2 1 | 1 2.

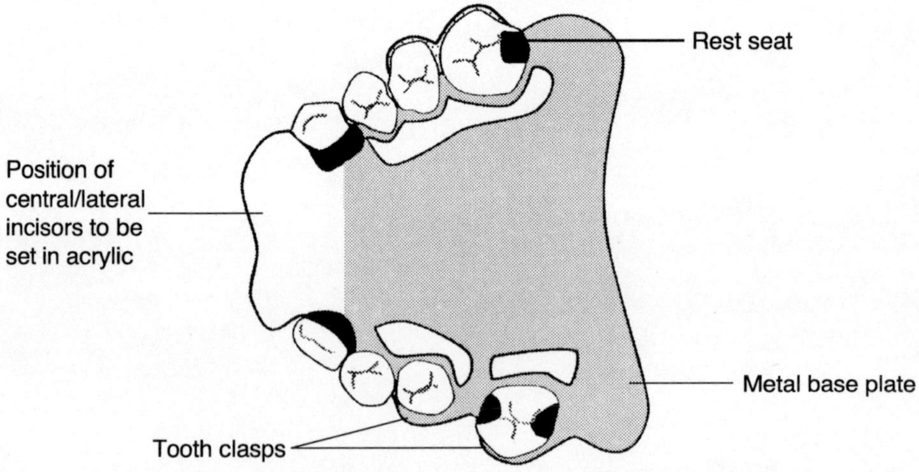

reason for retaining roots is to prevent bone resorption occurring. If suitable teeth such as canines or incisors, especially in the lower arch, are suitable for retaining, then after root canal treatment has been carried out and the crowns removed these roots can be left and used for support for the overlying denture.

Root canals can also be utilised for the provision of precision attachments in order to gain further retention and support of the overlying dentures. Various manufactured devices, such as studs, etc, can be utilised with the male part fitted into the remaining root and the female part incorporated into the acrylic of the dentures. The retained roots must be kept scrupulously clean as there is a tendency for rapid decay to occur if oral hygiene is poor, and therefore regular visits for reinforcement of oral hygiene are important.

PRECISION ATTACHMENTS

There are a number of devices, known as precision attachments, which are incorporated into dentures and remaining teeth to provide increased retention. A certain degree of skill is needed to remove them for cleaning and servicing. One example of such attachments is the dove tail joint, where the male attachment is incorporated into the denture framework and the female part is incorporated into a gold or porcelain-bonded-to-metal crown adjacent to the area where the teeth are to be replaced. Other devices include spring loaded clips, ball and socket attachments, etc. There are numerous attachments on the market with many minor variations in construction. These attachments incorporated into dentures and into crown and bridgework require great skill and technical expertise in order to reconstruct the patient's mouth.

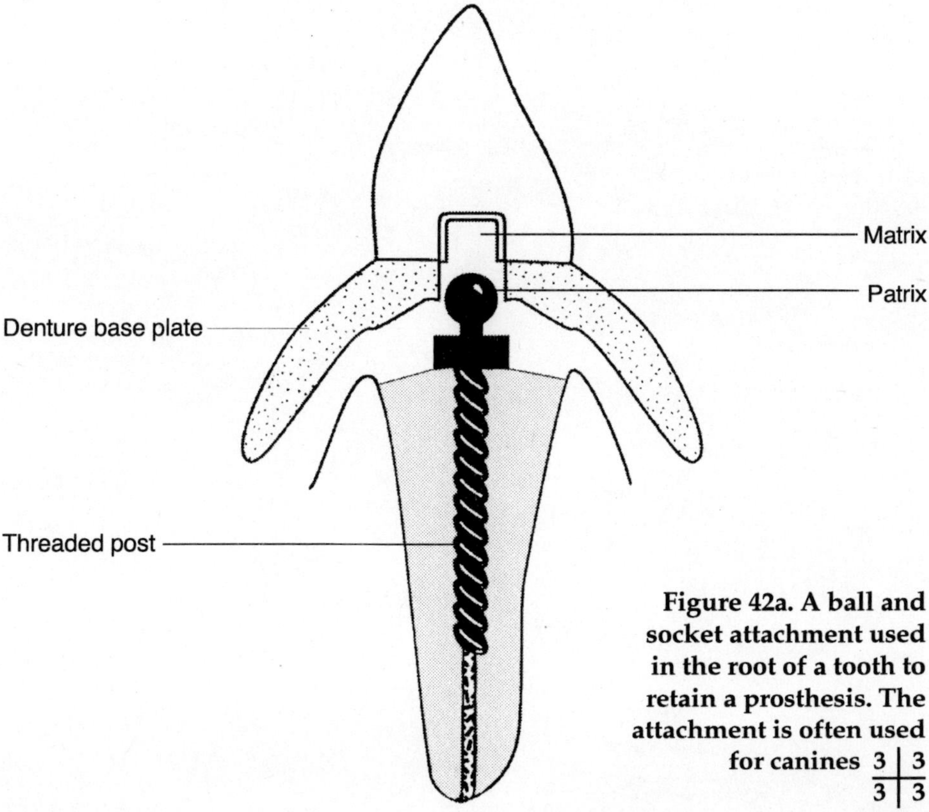

Figure 42a. A ball and socket attachment used in the root of a tooth to retain a prosthesis. The attachment is often used for canines $\frac{3|3}{3|3}$

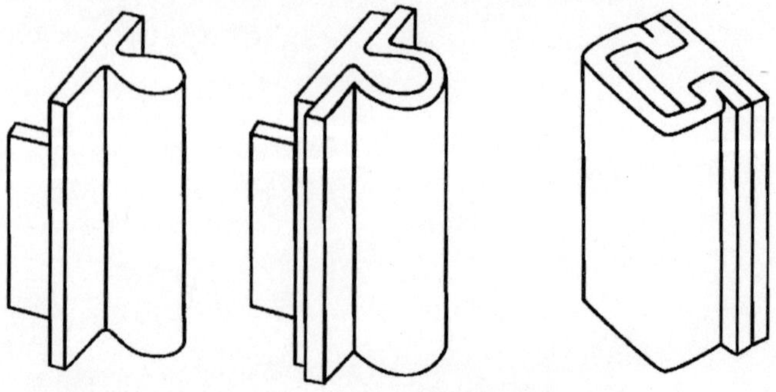

Figure 42b (above). Factory-made precision attachments incorporated into crowns and prostheses. Many are spring-loaded.

Figure 42c (below). Provision of a gold bar to acquire further retention and stability for a prosthesis.

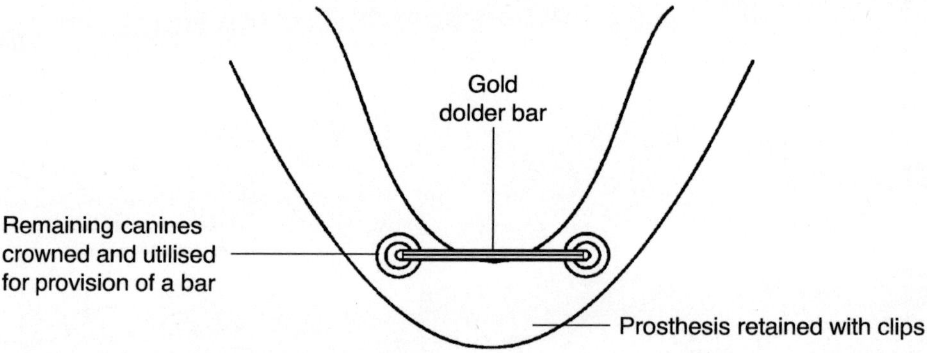

CHAPTER THIRTEEN

CHILDREN'S DENTISTRY (PAEDODONTICS)

The dental care of children is provided, for the most part, by the general dental practitioner under a capitation scheme. Children are also seen within the Community Dental Service and, for certain procedures, by the hospital service. The latter is usually involved in the care of children with underlying medical problems or special requirements.

COMMUNITY DENTAL SERVICE

The Community Dental Service was initially set up as a means of bringing dental health to children of school age. In its original form it consisted of dentists who would go into schools and examine large numbers of children in order to screen out those requiring dental treatment. These children would then be given letters advising their parents that they should be seen by their local dentist. Where this was not possible for various reasons, the Community Dental Service undertook the treatment themselves. The remit of community dental health has been extended to include pregnant and nursing mothers and various other groups, particularly children and adults with handicaps. In recent times, more and more children are being treated in the general dental practice environment as part of the family group. The Community Dental Services are now taking on a role in epidemiology and increasing their part in treating handicapped and other disadvantaged groups. They are also taking part in the management of the dental services in the community at large.

DENTAL THERAPISTS (AUXILIARIES)

These are a group of practitioners who have undergone a shortened training course which enables them to carry out certain procedures. The scope of their practice is strictly limited and, for the most part, revolves around simple restorations in primary teeth, ie those teeth which are to be shed. They are small in number and exist mainly in dental hospitals where they have a high workload treating children.

In essence, children's dentistry is no different to that in the adult. It highlights the training of children in maintaining their oral hygiene and educating them about dental diseases and their prevention. The restoration of carious primary teeth is essentially the same as that in adult teeth. Certain forms of treatment, eg advanced crown and bridgework, are not carried out in children. However, pre-formed stainless steel crowns are occasionally used in heavily restored teeth. Root canal treatment is also impractical for the most part in deciduous teeth due to the shape of their root canals. Therefore, when necessary the teeth are often devitalised and left in situ without root fillings or have the pulp chamber amputated (pulpotomy).

The most important aspect of treatment in children, however, is the preventative advice and procedures. These include the provision of fluoride treatment, as detailed below, and the sealing of the fissures in the occlusal (biting) surface of the teeth with composite materials in a process similar in concept to the undersealing of a car against corrosion.

FLUORIDE

There is now a considerable weight of evidence to show that teeth pick up fluoride from the environment. Providing it is of sufficient quantity to saturate the outer layers of the tooth it increases the resistance of the teeth to decay by a considerable degree. The saturation of teeth with fluoride occurs naturally over a number of years, which is partly why adults are less prone to decay than children.

In order to accelerate this process there have been various methods of adding fluoride artificially. The most controversial of these is adding fluoride to drinking water. It has been well demonstrated that, in the concentrations proposed, there are no harmful effects. But this has not become a widespread practice since some sections of the community find it unacceptable that anything should be added to the drinking water. This leaves people with no choice as to whether they take it or not.

Having said this, other chemicals such as chlorine are compulsorily added for health reasons. Fluoride has been applied directly in high concentrations by dentists for a number of years, but without doubt the most significant method of fluoride application in recent years has been its addition to toothpaste. Somewhere in the region of 95% of all toothpaste used in the UK is fluoridated, and it is thought that this has been one of the major factors in reducing the level of dental decay.

CHAPTER FOURTEEN

ORTHODONTICS

Orthodontics is the specialty which encompasses the moving of teeth using various appliances to improve the function and/or aesthetics of the teeth.

Although simple orthodontic procedures are carried out by general dental practitioners, the more complex orthodontic cases are treated by either specialist practitioners or the hospital orthodontic service. The appliances that are used may be simply divided into:

(a) removable appliances – which are made of a plastic (acrylic) base with various metal springs and clips and are worn for the majority of the day, but which may be removed for cleaning purposes; and

(b) fixed appliances – which involve the cementing of various brackets and bands to the teeth in such a way that they may not be removed on a day to day basis.

In both cases, tooth movement is obtained by applying forces via wires and springs, while the appliance as a whole is retained by other teeth. Occasionally, extra anchorage is required and extra-oral traction is supplied wearing headgear to which are attached wires and elastics protruding from the mouth.

The scope of orthodontics is wide. It ranges from the simple movement of one tooth into a cosmetically better position in a short time using a simple appliance, to major tooth movements involving the majority of teeth and using fixed appliances taking as long as two years. The specialists who undertake the more complex procedures are practitioners who have undergone a further period of postgraduate training leading to the award of a diploma or membership in orthodontics of one of the royal colleges. They may then practice as specialist practitioners or may undergo a further period of higher training in order to achieve hospital consultant status.

There are two other areas in which orthodontics is relevant. Firstly in orthognathic surgery, where deformities of the jaws are treated surgically but, for the best results, often require movement of the teeth either prior to or following surgery. Equally, many patients who seek simple movement of the teeth into a better functional or cosmetic position require movement so large as to be impractical. These patients may also require movement of part or all of the jaws, involving major surgery carried out under hospital conditions with a maxillofacial surgeon and an orthodontist.

The second major area in which orthodontics has an input is in the treatment of cleft palate patients. The treatment of these patients is complex and involves many specialties (eg maxillofacial surgeons, orthodontists, restorative dentists, plastic surgeons, paediatricians, ear nose and throat surgeons and speech therapists). However, following the initial closure of the cleft itself a large burden of the work falls on the orthodontist, and in most areas the orthodontist will be the team leader or at least play a prominent role in the long term treatment.

CHAPTER FIFTEEN

ORAL SURGERY

Traditionally, oral surgery has composed that part of dental surgery that involves the removal of teeth, or their remnants, and various pathological lesions from within the mouth. It has also included operations on the teeth themselves and the treatment of traumatic injuries in and around the mouth.

Because of their expert knowledge of teeth, and in particular the way in which teeth meet together and function, dentists in the past were able to use this expertise in the treatment of more major fractures of the jaws themselves, and gradually as the hospital-based specialty of oral surgery developed, practitioners specialised and became more expert in treating a wide variety of pathology and trauma around the mouth and jaws. In recent years the amount and scope of this type of surgery has increased dramatically. The hospital-based specialty of oral surgery has grown to encompass the field known as maxillofacial surgery, and the majority of hospitals in this country now have a department of oral and maxillofacial surgery.

This extended role has meant that the current requirements to enter the specialty include both a medical and dental qualification and surgical training. The majority of procedures carried out in these units are outside the scope of general dental practice and are not considered in detail in this book. However, many of the procedures carried out are of a more minor nature and are suitable for treatment with local anaesthesia, with or without sedation, and are often carried out by general dental practitioners in the community. These oral surgical procedures will be discussed in more detail, although some reference will be made to jaw fractures and their treatment. Further details of the relationships between the general practitioner and the oral and maxillofacial surgeon and their responsibilities will be discussed.

ORAL SURGERY IN DENTAL PRACTICE

This includes the removal of teeth which may be erupted, buried or impacted, and the removal of fragments of teeth which may have been left behind from previous extractions. Small bone cysts may be removed by some practitioners. Those involved in orthodontics (see Chapter 14) will often undertake procedures to expose buried teeth and may bond chains onto these teeth for attachment to orthodontic appliances in order to move them.

Biopsies of soft tissue lesions and the repair of minor trauma to the lips and tongue may also be carried out, together with some procedures altering the shape of edentulous ridges during the preparation for denture wearing.

Finally, procedures on the teeth themselves, such as apicectomies and hemisectomies, may also be carried out. These will be discussed more fully below.

Extraction of teeth (exodontia)

The removal of teeth has traditionally been the most important function of a dental surgeon. Fortunately, due to improved education, public awareness and dental expertise, this event is becoming increasingly rare.

Although one must be on the dental register to practice dentistry, the removal of teeth is also permitted under certain circumstances by registered medical practitioners.

The first stage of the procedure is to render the patient free of pain. The commonest way of achieving this is by local anaesthetic, although other modalities such as hypnosis or general anaesthesia may be used, as previously discussed. Teeth are traditionally removed with dental forceps. There is a large range designed to suit the shape of individual teeth in the mouth, although the instrument used in each instance is largely determined by personal preference and by experience. Teeth are also removed using instruments called elevators, which are specialised levers used to either loosen or in some cases remove the teeth by levering against the bone in which they are situated. Various designs are available, eg Warwick James, Cryers, Couplands.

During the extraction of teeth the dental surgeon is obliged to take all reasonable care not to damage adjacent teeth or soft tissue, and that includes the soft tissue of the lips. Occasionally a minor injury to these structures is unavoidable, depending on many factors such as the size and shape of the teeth and of the mouth itself, the difficulty of the extraction and, most importantly, patient co-operation. Sometimes very large forceps need to be applied, and the dental surgeon needs to be aware of the possibility of jaw fractures, especially in older patients with relatively brittle bone, and of damage to adjacent structures such as nerves and, in the upper jaw, the maxillary sinus.

Having removed the tooth it must be established whether the whole tooth has been removed or whether parts have been retained, which occasionally happens in spite of the best care. A decision on whether to remove any remains or whether they are safe to leave depends on the individual circumstances and the patient. Following removal the inevitable bleeding must be stopped, and this is usually achieved by pressure using a pack held in place for approximately 10 minutes (haemostasis). Careful post-operative instructions are given to patients explaining how they should look after the wound and what they should do if they experience excessive pain or recurrent bleeding. In occasional circumstances a stitch (suture) may need to be applied. There is now a contractual obligation on dentists to provide follow up care for their patients, including 'out of hours advice and treatment as necessary'.

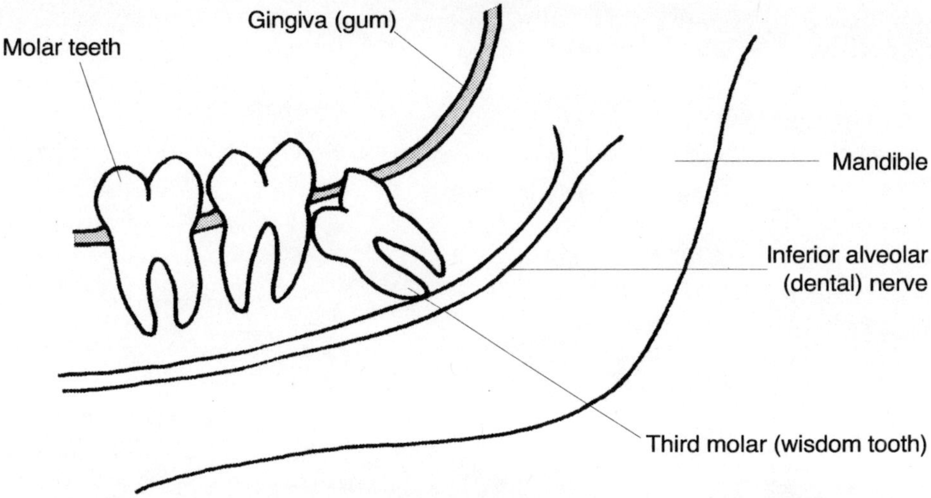

Figure 43. The impacted wisdom tooth.

Surgical removal of teeth

In some instances the teeth may be buried or impacted against other teeth. This prevents the straightforward extraction of such teeth, and some form of surgical removal is indicated. It is proposed in this section to go through a surgical procedure in simple terms, describing the basic techniques and surgical instruments along the way. The other common surgical procedures will then be described, simply highlighting the difference from the standard surgical procedure.

Removal of an impacted third molar (wisdom tooth)

Teeth are described as impacted when they impinge on other teeth, and as a result are unable to erupt properly into the mouth. There are various causes of this. Third molars (wisdom teeth) are the commonest teeth to fail to erupt into the mouth due to impaction (Figure 43). They often need to be removed due to either symptoms of pressure or more usually the symptoms of infection. The first step in removing an impacted third molar, as in any procedure, is to discuss the treatment fully with the patient, outlining the alternatives and obtaining detailed consent for the procedure to be carried out. The taking of X-rays is important for clinical assessment. At the start of the surgical procedure it needs to be established that the correct patient notes and X-rays are married together and that all the equipment necessary for the procedure is at hand.

Adequate anaesthesia of one form or another must be established before the procedure may begin. Initially, the area to be operated on must be exposed by means of an incision through the gum using a scalpel. A gum flap is then lifted using an instrument termed a periosteal elevator (of which there are many designs).

Having exposed the site, the soft tissues may be held out of the way using one of the many designs of retractor, which also protects surrounding structures. The next stage is to uncover the tooth by removing a sufficient amount of bone using either a bur in a dental motor or chisels (Figure 44). It is important to protect the surrounding tissue, particularly when using a motor, and specific mention of nerve damage related to this is made below. During bone removal with a bur it is important to irrigate the area with a sterile liquid such as saline to keep the tissues cool, thus preventing heat damage to the bone and washing away debris. Following bone removal it may be necessary to divide the tooth by use of the motor and bur or an instrument called an osteotome.

The tooth may then be removed using elevators or forceps, as mentioned in the description on removal of teeth. The sharp edges of bone are smoothed with either a bur or file and the area thoroughly irrigated. Closure is then obtained using a stitch (suture). The suture is held securely in an instrument called a needle-holder, and the gum is handled using toothed forceps.

There are various types of stitch material. The most commonly used in general dental practice is still silk, although many people now use a material termed catgut which is actually made from sheep's intestines. This is slowly resorbed by the body and therefore does not need to be removed. Modern synthetic materials are available which may be either of the dissolving or non-dissolving type. Non-dissolving sutures need to be removed, normally 5–7 days after insertion.

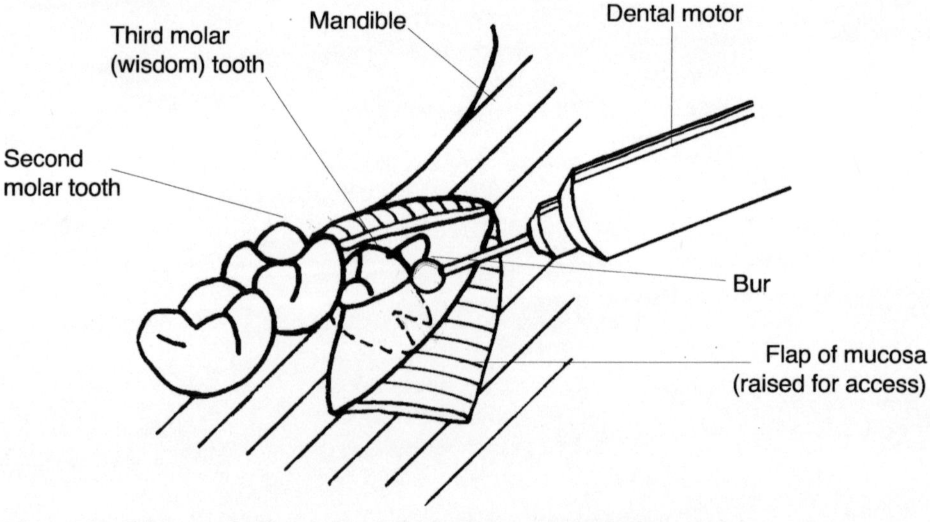

Figure 44. The surgical approach to an impacted wisdom tooth.

Removal of a cyst

A cyst is simply a fluid-filled space lined with a skin-like tissue. Those that are in the soft tissues may be simply excised; those within the bone need to be exposed in a similar way as described for exposing an impacted tooth. They may then be enucleated, which means removing them from within their bony cavity and closing the mucosa over them. Occasionally it may be better to marsupialise them, which is a process whereby a window is made and the lining of the cyst is simply attached to the mucosa, leaving the defect open to the mouth. This is then kept clean over a period of time during which the cavity hopefully gets smaller.

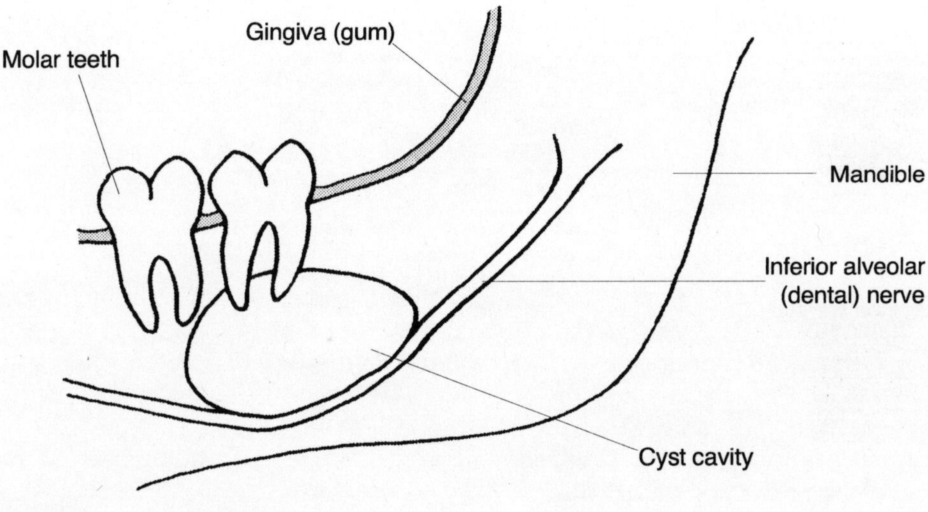

Figure 45. A cyst in the jaw.

Apicectomy

An apicectomy is simply the removal of the apex of the tooth root. This is sometimes necessary when root canal treatment (see Chapter 10) fails and infection persists around the apex of the tooth. The approach is similar to that described for an impacted tooth, and once the apex is exposed it is removed to leave the rest of the tooth in situ. A standard cavity is prepared at the end of the root canal in the remaining tooth, and a filling material such as amalgam placed into it ('retrograde root filling'). The wound is then closed in the usual way (Figure 46).

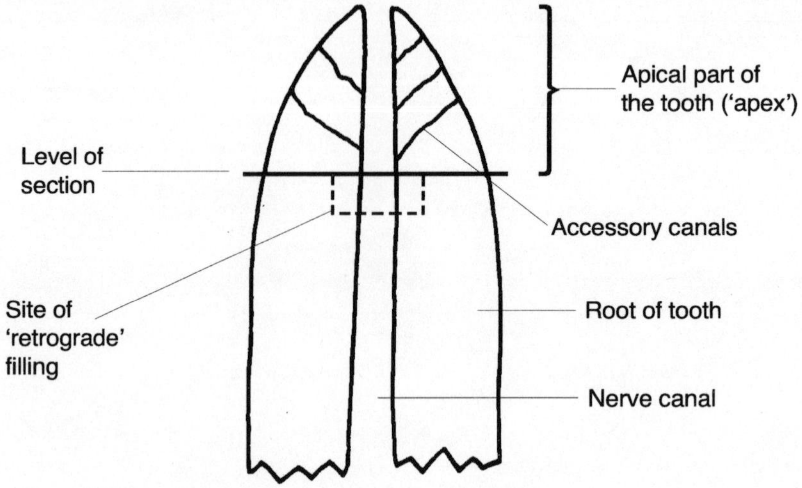

Figure 46. The apex of a tooth.

After care

Following any surgical procedure, it is important to explain to the patient about the care of the surgical wound. They are instructed to avoid hot drinks or food, alcohol and exercise. These three factors increase blood flow and therefore increase the risk of bleeding. Bleeding can be controlled in the majority of cases using a bite pad for 15–20 minutes. It is occasionally necessary to take further measures to stop bleeding, including the use of stitching or packing of the wound.

It is quite usual to develop swelling following any surgical procedure, and in the head and neck this can be quite dramatic. Bruising may also occur, and its existence is not necessarily an indication of the extent of the surgery. While it is normal to experience discomfort following surgery to the mouth, this is usually controllable using simple analgesics obtainable without prescription. It is sometimes necessary to provide stronger painkillers, but each case needs to be assessed on its merits. In some circumstances antibiotics may also be required to prevent or control infection.

Complications

Other than pain, swelling, bleeding and infection, most complications relate to damage of adjacent structures during the surgery itself. Bleeding, pain and swelling have been mentioned above, and infection is prevented simply by attention to oral hygiene and in selected cases by the prescribing of antibiotics.

The most important structures that may be damaged during surgical procedures are nerves. Whereas most of the structures which may be damaged will heal, nerve damage may be permanent. Those nerves particularly at risk in surgery of the jaws are:

(a) inferior dental nerve, which supplies sensation to the lower teeth and also, via its mental nerve branch, half of the lower lip; and

(b) the lingual nerve which supplies sensation to the tongue.

It is during removal of third molars that injury is most likely to take place. Damage to the lingual nerve may occur if the inner plate of the lower jaw is breached during bone removal, especially when using a bur, as the nerve lies directly on the bone at this point. Some surgeons place a retractor between the bone and the mucosa on this side of the jaw to prevent just such an injury, but the placing of the instrument itself may damage the nerve.

The inferior dental nerve runs just beneath the lower wisdom tooth and its position is variable. It may be well away from or touching the tooth. In extreme circumstances the nerve may run through a groove within the tooth, and there are recorded cases of the nerve running through the tooth substance itself (Figure 43).

Because of the difficulty in assessing the exact position, even with X-rays, it is an accepted risk of the procedure of removing a third molar that damage to this nerve and the lingual nerve may occur. Injury to these nerves results in loss of or altered sensation in the area supplied by them, ie the anterior third of the tongue for the lingual and the lower lip for the inferior dental. It is imperative that patients are warned of this risk before embarking on surgery.

The other important complication of surgery to the jaws is fracture. In the upper jaw this is a very rare phenomenon and usually only relates to a fracture through the small piece of bone behind the last molar tooth, called the tuberosity, which occasionally occurs when removing the last molar tooth itself. The consequences of this are minor and, provided it is recognised and dealt with at the time, no untoward effects are likely to occur.

When removing lower teeth, particularly molars and especially third molars, there is a risk of jaw fracture. Although this risk is usually very small indeed, unless excessive force is used there are cases, particularly where the jaws are thin and in old people where the bone is brittle, where jaw fracture may occur even though the greatest care is taken. In cases noted to be at risk a warning is normally given. However, even in the apparently low risk case it is possible, even with the best care, for a fracture to occur. Provided this complication is recognised, it may be dealt with satisfactorily. Those cases where a fracture occurs but is not detected are those which may give rise to medico-legal proceedings at a later date.

When using sharp or rotating instruments within the mouth, there is also a risk of damage to adjacent soft tissues, particularly when the patient is awake and may move unexpectedly. This can occur in spite of the best precautions, and the advice given to dental surgeons is that any such incidents should be explained to the patient, a record made in the notes of the occurrence, and suitable aftercare provided.

Referral to hospital

It is always open to an individual practitioner to refer complex cases to a hospital-based oral surgeon. Most dentists are well aware of their capabilities and limitations, and will err on the side of caution and refer all but those cases they feel they can competently handle. Inevitably, there are occasions when a procedure is assessed as being straightforward but, when attempted, is found to be complex. In such cases the dentists will normally contact the local hospital for immediate advice and, if necessary, transfer.

The training in oral surgery varies between dental schools. However, many dental surgeons will undergo periods of postgraduate training in hospitals. This means that, within the country as a whole, there is a wide variation in the degree of training in oral surgery. It is for this reason that it is impossible to lay down exact criteria for what is an acceptable procedure in practice and what should be referred, and it must always be up to the individual practitioner to assess his or her own capabilities. The hospital oral surgery service, however, has strict criteria for training. A prescribed period of training must be undertaken, firstly of a general nature, during which time the examination of the Fellowship in Dental Surgery of one of the royal colleges of surgeons needs to be obtained. A period of higher specialist training must then be undertaken before an accreditation certificate is awarded in the specialty of oral and maxillofacial surgery. In recent years, the addition of a medical degree and a surgical fellowship of one of the royal colleges has also become mandatory, and it would not now be possible to be accredited without these qualifications.

Consent

Informed consent must always be sought for any procedure. It has always been the case in routine dentistry that, although consent has not been obtained in writing, it is assumed when patients allows themselves to be treated. A verbal explanation of the procedure is always given first. Many dental surgeons, however, obtain express consent before extraction of teeth or surgical procedures.

In hospital practice it has always been mandatory to obtain written consent for a procedure under general anaesthesia, although the practice under local anaesthesia has varied widely between different hospitals. Consent forms are currently undergoing change. Most hospitals are developing a more complex and wide-ranging consent form which it is necessary to complete before any procedure under local or general anaesthetic is carried out. Although the use of consent forms is standard procedure, it is still necessary to demonstrate that adequate consent has indeed been given, and the presence of a signed document does not absolve a practitioner of his responsibilities to give a full and frank explanation of the procedure intended and the risks involved.

Collagen replacement therapy

A small number of dental surgeons looking for new avenues of treatment have recently become involved in the process of injecting collagen into the tissues of the face in order to eliminate, or at least reduce, wrinkles, skin creases and a variety of other features of the normal ageing process.

Bovine collagen (derived from Hereford beef cattle) is injected into the soft tissues along the line of the facial discrepancy. The collagen comes in sterile syringes with varying viscosities, depending on the severity of the furrow or wrinkle to be eliminated. The treatment has been accepted by the General Dental Council as long as the collagen therapy is undertaken by a practitioner who has had sufficient training. As the treatment is relatively new in the UK, the medico-legal aspects of the treatment are still under discussion.

Fractures of the jaw

Fractures of the jaws are usually associated with excessive trauma being applied. The commonest causes are assault, road traffic accidents and sporting injuries. Occasionally the jaw may be fractured by minimal force if it has been weakened previously by disease or surgery.

The upper jaw (maxilla) is not commonly fractured, but when it is there are often extensive or multiple fractures involving other parts of the facial skeleton associated with it. The fractures do, however, fall into a number of general patterns described by a surgeon in the last century, and named after him as Le Fort I, II and III-level fractures. (See Figure 45, page 100.)

The common fracture of the face is that of the cheek ('zygoma' or 'malar') bone. This is usually as a result of assault and may be associated with damage to the eye (Plate 7, *overleaf*).

Fractures involving the lower jaw (mandible) are also fairly common. They may be single, double and occasionally multiple. There is a risk of damage to the inferior dental nerve which runs in the bone, and when the fracture is displaced the teeth do not meet correctly (malocclusion).

The treatment as in all fractures is to realign the bones in their correct position and then to stabilise them in this position for as long as it takes to heal, commonly 4–6 weeks. Traditionally, jaws have been wired together to achieve this by passing wires around the teeth and then attaching the wires of one jaw to those of the other, with the teeth in the correct alignment.

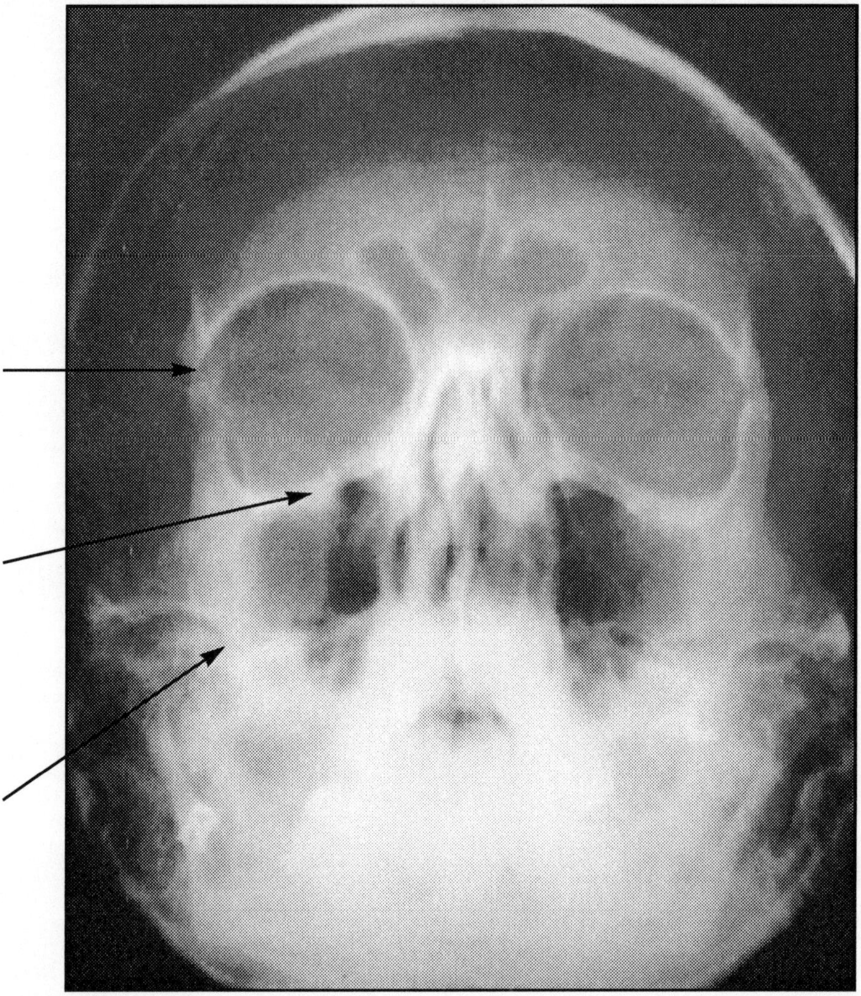

Plate 7. Occipito-mental radiograph of the head. The arrows indicate a fractured right molar (cheekbone).

More recently, however, plates and screws made of steel and more recently titanium have been used to fix the fracture directly and so avoid the need for wiring the jaws together with all the restrictions of eating that the method imposes.

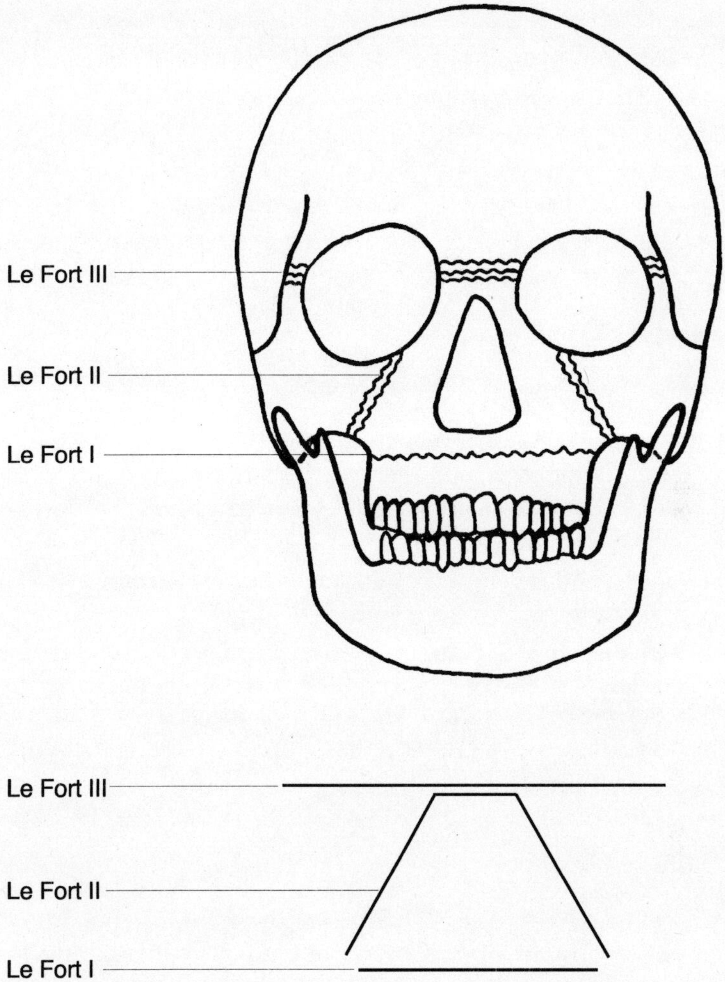

Figure 47. 'Le Fort' classification of common maxillary fractures (Le Fort I = low level; Le Fort II = pyramidal; Le Fort III = high level).

IMPLANTS

Implants are devices which are used to retain artificial parts of the body or even to replace various parts completely.

In the field of dentistry implants are used to support artificial teeth of one sort or another. This may be by providing an anchor for dentures or a scaffolding onto which bridgework can be attached.

Various methods and materials have been tried over many years and with various degrees of success, however, most had poor long term results and many had to be removed. Implants gradually fell out of use.

More recently a successful method of implanting material has been discovered and has now had a proven long term track record. This uses the principle of oseointegration. It was discovered that pure titanium had the unusual property of being accepted by the body when implanted in bone rather than exciting a reaction which would lead to rejection. The bone grew up to the titanium and the implant was said to have integrated in it.

It was then found that if a pure titanium post (abutment) was fixed to this implant and left protruding through the mucosa of the mouth that it did not get infected or work loose if it was looked after.

This led to the design and use of dental implants which although of various types all have in common the use of titanium as the material and a careful method of insertion. Once inserted they are left for 3–6 months to 'integrate' and only when this has occurred are they exposed to allow the attachment of the titanium abutment.

Once the abutment is in place bridges or dentures may be fixed to or retained by the implant.

Problems arise in placing these implants since they have to be of a reasonable size to be strong enough to take the strain imposed on them by the denture or bridge. Placing them into the upper or lower jaw without damaging the nerves, vessels and other anatomical obstructions therefore requires a sound knowledge, expertise and experience.

Most of the problems which give rise to litigation are concerned with damage to adjacent structures or to failure of the implant. Failure even in the best hands does occur although it should be in the order of a few percent only.

Implants are expensive and are not provided by the National Health Service routinely. Some health authorities will finance a few on chosen deserving patients and some are provided by charities for children and people who have suffered with oral cancer or trauma and have lost their teeth as a result. The majority, however, are provided in the private sector.

CHAPTER SIXTEEN

TEMPOROMANDIBULAR JOINT

The temporomandibular joint is the area just in front of the ear where the lower jaw hinges on the base of the skull. There are left and a right joints and each is individually divided into two sub-joints by a cartilaginous disc (meniscus). Provided the lower jaw is intact, the right and left joints cannot move in isolation. When closing, the final resting position of the joint is determined to some extent by the way in which the teeth, if present, meet together. For these reasons, this joint and its movements are complex and this, together with the proximity of other important structures, makes the diagnosis and treatment of problems in this area complex.

There is now a vast amount of literature on the diagnosis and treatment of the joint and associated problems in this area, and indeed, an eminent member of the oral surgery profession once stated that:

> 'Never in the field of oral surgery has so much been written by so many people on such a small topic.'

Pain and discomfort in this area may be caused by joint pathology, muscle problems or disease in the ear, parotid gland or other nearby structures. This is also an area subject to psychogenic pain. Because there are many conflicting views as to the real cause of the pain and discomfort in this area, it is a subject which gives rise to much debate and some highly individualistic treatments.

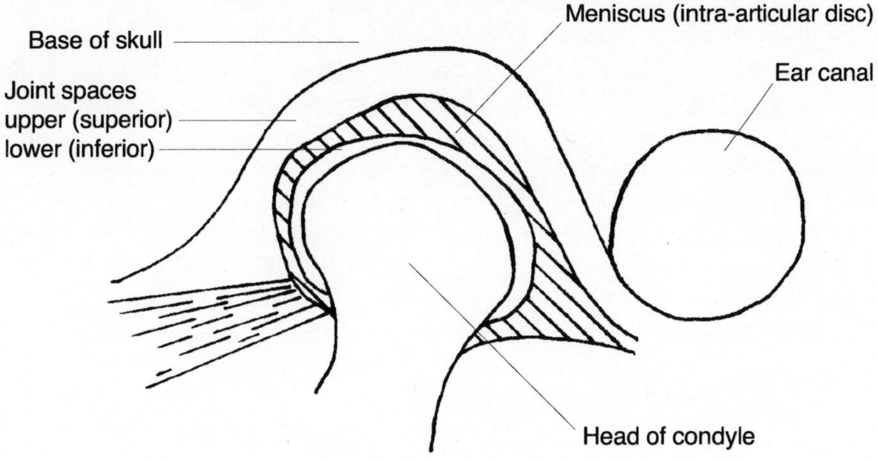

Figure 48. A cross-section of the temporomandibular joint.

The conditions can, however, be divided into two broad categories:

(a) facial arthromyalgia, which simply describes the symptoms, ie pain in the joint and surrounding muscles, by whatever cause; and

(b) functional defects of the joints themselves.

The functional defects due to a damaged joint or meniscus are more easily isolated as a group, although the treatment is complex and may involve surgical intervention. It is the area of facial arthromyalgia, however, where most of the controversy exists. A variety of terms have been used to describe the various signs and symptoms. Common terms include facial arthromyalgia and temporomandibular joint dysfunction syndrome.

Some people believe that the way the teeth meet has a large bearing on the cause of this, whereas others believe it has little or no relevance. Some believe it is simply due to the way in which the jaw is moved, and a large group of people believe that this is mainly a psychogenic problem exacerbated by stress and associated with other similar problems in various parts of the body. In addition to this, there are specific causes of joint problems such as trauma, tumours and arthritis, all of which need to be considered. There are undoubtedly links in terms of incidence with migraine, dysmenorrhoea, lower back pain and irritable bowel syndrome, although there is no direct connection between these various problems.

The treatment of facial arthromyalgia includes advice and reassurance, various drugs including painkillers and antidepressants, various appliances such as mouth guards, bite raising appliances and more specialised structures. X-rays of the joint, arthroscopy, interventional surgery and placebo treatment are also undertaken. In the extensive literature there are good studies which have shown a placebo effect of as much as 30%, which makes the evaluation of any individual treatment very difficult.

The majority of treatments cause no long term harmful effects and therefore problems do not arise from them. Interventional surgery is used for a number of specific reasons and has varying degrees of success. The commonest problems that result in litigation relate to treatments which alter the way the teeth meet, since any major alterations involving crowns, bridgework and grinding of teeth in order to treat this condition obviously have a permanent effect, and if it is unsuccessful or if the symptoms are exacerbated the patient will be unhappy. This is a highly controversial area and wide debate exists within dentistry about the effectiveness of such treatments.

APPENDIX

Societies and organisations

BDS	British Dental Association
GDPA	General Dental Practitioners Association
FHSA	Family Health Services Authority
GDC	General Dental Council
RCS	Royal College of Surgeons (Eng) of England (Ed) of Edinburgh (I) of Ireland
RCPS	Royal College of Physicians and Surgeons (Glasgow)

Qualifications

LDS	Licentiate in dental surgery
BDS (BChD)	Bachelor of dental surgery
MDS	Master of dental surgery
DGDPRCS	Diploma in general dental practice – RCS
DRDRCS	Diploma in restorative dentistry – RCS
MRDRCS	Membership in restorative dentistry – RCS
MGDSRCS	Membership in general dental surgery – RCS
DOrthRCS	Diploma in orthodontics – RCS
MOrthRCS	Membership in orthodontics – RCS
DDPHRCS	Diploma in dental public health – RCS
MCCDRCS	Member in clinical community dentistry – RCS
FFDRCS	Fellow of faculty of dentistry – RCS (Dublin)
FDSRCS	Fellowship in dental surgery – RCS
MSc	Master of science (crown and bridgework, prosthetics, endodontics, periodontology, etc)

Abbreviations

AIDS	Acquired immune deficiency syndrome
AUG	Acute ulcerative gingivitis
BDJ	*British Dental Journal*
DDO	District Dental Officer
DPB	Dental Practice Board
DPF	Dental Practitioners Formulary
DRO	Dental Reference Officer

DSA	Dental Surgery Assistant
EOT	Extra-oral traction (orthodontics)
F/-	Full upper denture
F/F	Full upper and full lower denture
-/F	Full lower denture
FGC	Full gold crown
GI	Gold inlay
HBV	Hepatitis B virus
HIV	Human immunodeficiency virus
MO	Mesial occlusal
DO	Disto occlusal
MOD	Mesial occlusal distal – cavity or filling
OPG	Orthopantomogram X-ray
P/-	Partial upper denture
P/P	Partial upper and lower dentures
-/P	Partial lower denture
PBC/VMK	Porcelain-bonded-to-metal crown
PJC	Porcelain jacket crown
CPITN	Community periodontal index of treatment needs

BIBLIOGRAPHY

Chapter 1

Hillam, Christine (ed), *The Roots of Dentistry* (*British Dental Journal*, 1990).

Chapter 2

BDA, *Health and Safety Law for Dental Practice* (advice sheet A3, September 1993).

BDA, *The Control of Cross-infection in Dentistry* (advice sheet A12, July 1991).

BDA, *Practice Inspection* (advice sheet B7, March 1992).

Wood, Peter R, *The Dentist's Guide to Cross Infection Control* 2nd edition (Guildford: George Warman Ltd, September 1993).

Chapter 3

Grant, *Atlas of Anatomy* 9th edition (Williams and Wilkins, 1991).

Gray's Textbook of Anatomy 38th edition (Churchill Livingstone, 1995).

Chapter 4

Scott, JH and Symons, NBB, *Introduction to Dental Anatomy* 9th edition (Churchill Livingstone, 1982).

Wheeler, RC and Ash, MM, *Dental Anatomy, Physiology and Occlusion* 5th edition (Saunders, 1992).

Chapter 6

Muir's Textbook of General Pathology 13th edition (Edward Arnold, 1992).

Spector, WG, *Introduction to General Pathology* 3rd edition (Churchill Livingstone, 1989).

Chapter 7

Berns, Joel M, *Understanding Periodontal Disease* (Quitessence, 1993).

Cawson, RA, *Essentials of Dental Surgery and Pathology* 5th edition (Churchill Livingstone, 1991).

Strahan, JD and Waite, IM, *A Colour Atlas of Periodontology* (Wolfe Medical Publications, 1978).

Chapter 8

Whitwam, G (ed), *Day Case Anaesthesia and Sedation* (Blackwell Scientific Publications, 1994).

Chapter 9

Department of Health, *Management, Preservation, Retention and Destruction of Records: Responsibility of Health Authorities Under the Public Records Act* (DoH, HC89 (20), 1989).

DHSS, *Radiological Protection in Dental Practice* (London: DHSS, 1988).

Health and Safety at Work Act 1974 (London: HMSO, 1974).

Living with Radiation (London: HMSO, 1986).

National Radiology Protection Board, Health and Safety Executive, Department of Health, *Popumet 1988 – Guidance Notes for the Protection of Persons Against Ionising Radiations Arising from Medical and Dental Use* (London: HMSO, 1988).

Chapter 10

Kidd, EAM and Smith, BGN, *Pickard's Manual of Operative Dentistry* 6th edition (Oxford Medical Publication, 1991).

Mumford, JM and Jedynakiewicz, NM, *Principles of Endodontics* (Quintessence, 1988).

Smith, BGN, *Planning and Making Crowns and Bridges* 2nd edition (Martin Dunitz, 1990).

Chapter 11

Neill, DJ and Nairn, RI, *Complete Denture Prosthetics* 3rd edition (Wright, 1990).

Neill, DJ and Walter, JD, *Partial Denture Prosthetics* 2nd edition (Blackwell Scientific, 1983).

Chapter 13

Andlaw, RJ and Rock, WP, *A Manual of Paedodontics* (Churchill Livingstone, 1988).

Chapter 14

Jones and Oliver (eds), *Walther and Houston's Orthodontic Notes* 5th edition (Wright, 1994).

Chapter 15

Howe, G, *Minor Oral Surgery* 3rd edition (Wright, 1985).

McGovern, DA, *Atlas of Minor Oral Surgery* (M Dunitz, 1989).

Rowe and Williams, *Maxillofacial Injuries* 2nd edition (Churchill Livingstone, 1994).

Chapter 16

Gray, RJM, Davies, SJ and Quayle, AA, *Temporomandibular Disorders: a Clinical Approach* (*British Dental Journal*, 1995).

INDEX

Page numbers in *italics* indicate a figure or table respectively, appearing away from its page